Challenges 1

Reading and Vocabulary for Academic Success

CYNTHIA A. BOARDMAN
Spring International Language Center
University of Arkansas, Fayetteville

LAURIE BARTON
Orange Coast College

Ann Arbor
The University of Michigan Press

Published in the United States of America
The University of Michigan Press
Manufactured in the United States of America

Printed on acid-free paper

ISBN-13: 978-0-472-03441-3

2015 2014 2013 2012 4 3 2 1

Acknowledgments

Our first debt of gratitude must go to ESL editor Laura LeDréan, who paired us as co-authors in 2005. She had a hunch that we would work well together, and she was right. With Laura's encouragement and guidance, we developed a prospectus for a series of reading books and searched for a publisher. This was, at times, a daunting process.

This is where our second debt of gratitude comes in. The University of Michigan Press recognized the merits of our prospectus and offered us a contract in 2009. We gratefully acknowledge Kelly Sippell at Michigan for her interest in our series and professional support. Kelly has offered helpful insight while respecting our autonomy as authors. We look forward to working with her as we develop the second and third books in the *Challenges* series.

Grateful acknowledgment is given to the following authors, publishers, and individuals for permission to reprint previously published materials.

Pocket Books for excerpt from *El Camino: A Journey of the Spirit* by Shirley Maclaine, from pages 4–5, 11–12, 145–147, 175–295. Copyright © 2000.

ThinkStock.com for photos.

Contents

To the Student

Welcome to *Challenges 1: Reading for Academic Success.* In this textbook, you will practice the strategies and skills that will help you become a better reader in English. Each of the eight units focuses on 16 useful academic vocabulary words as it explores one topic by reading two texts. You will have a chance to discuss your own ideas and use new vocabulary in your discussions. You will also learn new skills for building a stronger vocabulary and reading more quickly and effectively. When you complete this textbook, we hope you will know more about the art of reading and be ready to continue reading and learning as you pursue your English language goals.

To the Teacher

The purpose of each *Challenges* textbook is to help students become better readers through explicit teaching of reading skills and strategies that will break counter-productive habits, such as word-for-word translation. *Challenges 1* has eight units with two chapters in each. Each unit begins with an introduction to the topic—generally a one-page activity to activate students' interest and background knowledge.

Each chapter consists of six sections, each one designed to support students' understanding of a reading passage. **Getting Ready to Read** previews the specific reading topic the same way that the introduction previews the unit. **Vocabulary Preview** familiarizes students with the meaning of the eight vocabulary items highlighted in the chapter.

Skills

The **Reading Skills** section teaches one of three types: *basic reading skills, dictionary skills,* or *sentence-level grammar skills. Basic reading skills* include previewing, skimming, scanning, making inferences, and critical thinking as you read. These skills, which are essential to the development of a proficient reader, are addressed mostly in the first half of the book and practiced in later chapters. *Dictionary skills* address when to use a dictionary and look at different parts of an entry. The effective use of a dictionary is crucial to learning a language, and becoming familiar with an ESL/EFL learner dictionary can aid learners in ways other than understanding the meaning of a word. Learner dictionaries offer information not found in other dictionaries, such as usage notes, collocations, frequency of use, and register. *Sentence-level grammar skills* examine problematic grammatical structures, like coordinating conjunctions and transitions, cause-and-effect words and phrases, and pronoun references. These specific points are covered because they enhance sentence-level understanding and promote a grasp of understanding of how ideas are related within paragraphs.

These 16 different reading skills are labeled strategies and boxed. For example, a typical **Reading Skill** box includes the name of the skill, its purpose, examples, and explanations. After focusing on a reading skill, students practice using it in short exercises based on the reading passage.

Study Tip boxes contain helpful information on studying, such as where and when to study, ways to study for tests, and advice about joining study groups.

Post-Reading Activities

The **Reading Comprehension** exercise includes about ten questions on the content of the reading. These are objective questions (true/false and multiple choice) and open-ended questions to which students have to write a short answer. In later chapters, the answers require more thoughtful responses as higher-level reading skills (inference, distinguishing fact from opinion) are addressed. In **Discuss Your Ideas**, small groups of students talk about their thoughts and ideas about the events and/or dilemmas that are presented in the reading.

Vocabulary

A primary goal of *Challenges* is for students to increase their vocabulary by improving their word-learning skills and expanding each set of target words into related word forms. We agree with Keith S. Folse (*Vocabulary Myths,* 2004) that vocabulary acquisition and retention are critically important to second language learners and require a structured approach. Some textbooks emphasize using context clues to determine the meaning of unknown words. While we agree that paying attention to context is a valuable reading skill, our vocabulary exercises bypass this approach and directly support students' ability to recognize and comprehend the words encountered in each unit. Students will learn eight words in each chapter by focusing on their meanings and use in the reading passage and by retrieving the words in review exercises. An important aspect of vocabulary development is knowing all the ways a word is used. So students may know one meaning of the target vocabulary but not all. And, as Folse (2004) says, it can take as many as seven retrievals to learn a word. Students are also asked to use them in short writing assignments based on the readings. Each chapter also has a word form chart that includes the *most commonly used* forms of the targeted words. (It should be noted that ONLY the common forms are listed in the chart even though there may be other possible forms.) **Vocabulary Skill** boxes show students a variety of systematic approaches to organizing vocabulary acquisition, which will support students' independent word-learning skills as they progress beyond the scope of this book.

To determine which words to target, written passages were filtered through the Vocabulary Profiler developed by Laufer & Nation ("Vocabulary Size and Use," *Applied*

Linguistics, 1995) and adapted for the web by Tom Cobb at the University of Quebec at Montreal (www.lextutor.ca/vp/). Roughly half of the target words are from the list of 2,000 most frequent words used in English and the other half from the Academic Word List (Coxhead, "A New Academic Word List," *TESOL Quarterly*, 2000). We think that these results make a valuable list to which students can add other words that they want to learn.

Timed/Paced Reading

Because studies show that it's hard to comprehend a reading passage if students read it too slowly, activities for increasing reading speed are included at the end of each unit. Bell ("Extensive Reading: Speed and Comprehension," *The Reading Matrix Online Journal*, 2001) reports that a slow reader cannot keep in mind what he or she has read long enough to remember how it relates to what is being read at the moment. Therefore, it is important that English language learners try to read at a pace of at least 200 words per minute. This is especially important for academic students, but even casual reading requires a certain speed to comprehend, follow, and enjoy the reading. It is hard, though, for English language students to read without wanting to understand everything and therefore wanting to look up all the words that they don't understand in a passage. This, of course, greatly slows down the reading process and is actually a detriment to overall understanding. As a way of demonstrating to students that they can understand a lot more than they think when they read at a faster pace, two types of timed reading activities are presented in this book. Both types require students to read a short passage at a faster-than-normal pace and then answer some objective questions. Keeping track of the pace they read at and the score they get on the questions can dramatically show them that reading quickly does not detract from understanding. In fact, it may improve it.

The first type of activity, **timed reading**, is very common in language classes. Students set their own pace and try to increase the speed each time they read a passage. (See Appendix 2 for an explanation of the procedure.) The second type of activity, **paced reading**, can be considerably more effective at showing students that understanding the passage while reading at a faster rate is possible. In paced reading activities, the teacher sets the pace for the whole class and then pushes the students to read at a faster pace at regular intervals. (See Appendix 2 for an explanation of the procedure.) In both types of activities, students keep track of their reading speed and their comprehension score, but in paced reading, they can see that even though they are reading faster, their comprehension score remains the same or slowly increases once the new pace becomes somewhat comfortable.

Extra Materials

Because good readers read quickly, which demonstrates automaticity—a sign of fluency—a timed/paced reading has been added to each chapter. **Appendix 1** contains the questions for the timed/paced reading passages at the end of each unit.

Appendix 2, Increasing Reading Speed, explains the procedures for timed and paced reading for teachers and students. Included are charts for each type where students can keep track of their reading speed and comprehension score.

Appendix 3 is a list of the 128 targeted words in the textbook.

Teachers will find **Unit Review** activities online at www.press.umich.edu/esl/ that provide additional vocabulary activities, more opportunities for discussion, and a short reading journal assignment that encourages reflection as students relate the readings to their own experiences.

The goal in this series is to **challenge** students to become more skillful, independent readers and to provide a strong foundation that will serve them well as they pursue their goals. We welcome any comments or questions at esladmin@umich.edu.

UNIT 1

Street Performers

Street performers have been around for centuries. Today they are in most large cities in the world. They perform for people on the street. They usually have a basket or hat in front of them for money. If people like their performance, they put money in the basket.

Work with a classmate. Match the type of street performer in the left column with the description of the performance in the right column. Then discuss other kinds of street performers you've seen.

1. drummer	a. predicts information or events about a person's life
2. escape artist	b. tells a story or communicating with actions or gestures but not by using any words
3. fortune teller	c. frees oneself from handcuffs or restraints or traps such as boxes or cages
4. juggler	d. plays music
5. mime	e. throws several objects up in the air in a timed order to catch them and then throw them again without dropping any of the objects

CHAPTER

1

The Zip Code Man

Getting Ready to Read

How good is your memory? Try this experiment. Tell your classmate your telephone number. Then your classmate will tell you his or her telephone number. Do not write it down or save it. Each of you will try to remember the telephone number. Remember: you cannot write it down.

Vocabulary Preview

For each sentence, choose the word or phrase to match the meaning of the word in bold.

brings something to another place
enjoyable
make a picture
more or less
not average or typical
remember
a show
a system used to give or show information with signs or symbols

1. We have to **memorize** 25 vocabulary words for tomorrow's test.

   I think **memorize** means ______________________________.

2. My sister can **draw** animals very well. Her animals look real!

   I think **draw** means ______________________________.

3. When someone plays the guitar for other people, it is called a **performance.**

   I think **performance** means ______________________________.

4. I don't know how many people are in the crowd, but I can guess. There are **approximately** 45. There may be one or two more, but I think that's how many there are.

   I think **approximately** means ______________________________.

5. He **delivers** our office mail in the morning. The mail is on our desks before we eat lunch.

   I think **delivers** means ______________________________.

6. Steve writes **codes** for computer programs. The numbers tell the computer what to do.

   I think **codes** means ______________________________.

7. A clerk is a common type of job. A furniture tester is an **unusual** job.

   I think **unusual** means ______________________________.

8. The street performer was **entertaining.** I laughed a lot.

   I think **entertaining** means ______________________________.

Do you still know your classmate's telephone number?

Reading Skill

Skill	**Previewing**
Purpose	To get a general idea of the reading before you read
Explanation	Before you read an article, you should look at • **the title and subtitles** • **diagrams, charts, and tables** • **photographs and illustrations (drawings)** As you look at these, think about what they tell you about the article. Previewing doesn't take a very long time, but it gets you thinking about what you will read, and that can help you understand more when you read.

Previewing

Work with a classmate to preview the reading on pages 5 and 6 by discussing the answers to these questions.

1. What is the title? Can you guess what a "zip code man" is?
2. Look at the illustration. What is it? How is it related to the title?
3. Look at the photo. What is it? How is it related to the title?

Reading

The Zip Code Man

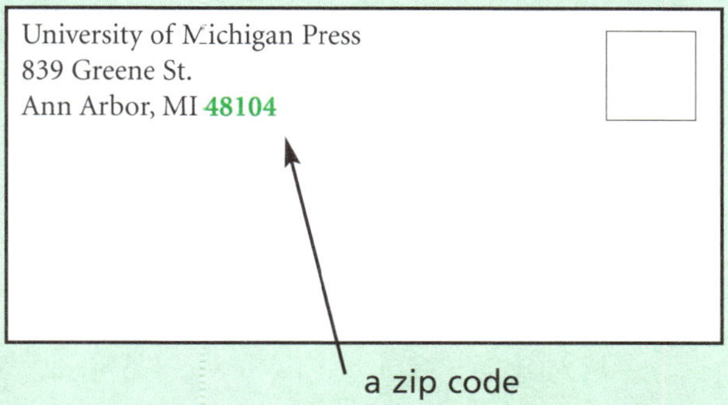

David Rosdeitcher is an **unusual** street performer. He stands on the street and asks people to tell him their zip **codes**. Then he tells them where they are from. Next, he asks other people to tell him their zip **codes**, and he also tells them the name of their cities. David can do this because he knows 40,000 zip **codes** of places in the United States.

What is a zip **code**? It is the number that you put at the end of your address. It is a number that tells what state and city you live in. The U.S. post office started using zip **codes** in 1963 to help with the **delivery** of mail. There are **approximately** 45,000 zip **codes**, but no one knows exactly how many there are. This is because the numbers are always changing.

Interestingly, David was born in the same year that the post office started using zip **codes**, 1963. When David was a child, he liked maps and numbers. In fact, when he was five, he named all the state capitals.* He started doing street **performances** in the 1980s when he was in college in New Orleans. He was a good juggler, and he could ride a unicycle. After college, he decided to move to Boulder, Colorado, but there were already many street jugglers in Boulder. David decided to use his good memory skills. He started to **memorize** zip **codes** in 1991 and then became the Zip **Code** Man.

*__capitals__—*n.* cities where a country's or state's main government is located

David usually does his work outside at a mall** in Boulder, Colorado. He stands on the street and begins to ask people what their zip **codes** are. He tells them where they are from, and then he names a good restaurant in their town. People are surprised that David is almost always correct. During his **performance**, he **draws** a big map of the United States on the ground. When he finishes the map, he asks more people for their zip **codes**. Then he asks them to stand on the map in the place where they live. When he has about 20 or 30 people on his map, he stops. Then, he points at each person and says the zip **code** and town of that person. People are surprised by his memory.

David is very happy being the Zip **Code** Man. He says, "I'm not always right, but I'm usually always **entertaining**." What else should a good street performer be?

****mall**—*n.* a place where there are a lot of stores and restaurants

Reading Comprehension

Circle the letter of the correct answer, or write a short answer.

1. What is a zip code?
   a. a place
   b. a number
   c. a name
2. No one knows the exact number of zip codes.
   a. true
   b. false
   c. The reading doesn't say.
3. David can memorize zip codes and
   a. the names of places
   b. the names of restaurants
   c. both a and b

4. David was a juggler in
   a. New Orleans
   b. Boulder
   c. both a and b

5. When David performs, he draws a map of
   a. Colorado
   b. the United States
   c. Boulder

6. During one performance, David memorizes
   a. 40,000 zip codes
   b. 20 or 30 zip codes
   c. more than 30 zip codes

7. David likes his job.
   a. true
   b. false
   c. The reading doesn't say.

8. What is unusual about David's job? ________________________________

   ____

Discuss Your Ideas

In small groups, discuss the answers to these questions. Be prepared to share your answers with the class.

1. Are you good at memorizing things? What things have you memorized?
2. Do you know anyone with an unusual ability? What can this person do?
3. Would you like to watch David perform? Why or why not?
4. What kinds of street performers are common in your culture?

STUDY TIP

Setting Goals

Good students think about why they are studying. They have goals. What are your goals for studying? Are they short-term goals? Are they long-term goals? Look at this list. Add your own goals at the bottom of the list.

1. I want to pass a test.
2. I want to write a paper.
3. I want to get an A in this class.
4. I want to graduate.
5. I want to get a good job.
6. ____________________
7. ____________________

Vocabulary Comprehension

With a classmate, fill in the empty boxes in the chart. Do not write anything in the boxes that have an X. You can use an English dictionary.

Nouns	Verbs	Adjectives	Adverbs
			approximately
code		X	X
delivery		X	X
	draw	X	X
1. 2.		entertaining	X
1. 2.	memorize		
1. performance 2.			X
X	X	unusual	

Matching

Match each word in the left column with its opposite meaning in the right column.

____	1. approximate	a. take
____	2. code (v.)	b. observe
____	3. deliver	c. forget
____	4. draw	d. common
____	5. entertain	e. erase
____	6. memorize	f. break down; crack
____	7. perform	g. bore
____	8. unusual	h. exact

Word Forms

For each sentence, change the incorrect word form in bold to the correct word form.

__________________ 1. The **entertainment** juggler juggled six pans at one time.

__________________ 2. I love to study art, but my **draw** isn't very good.

__________________ 3. People don't have to **memorization** phone numbers any more because cell phones keep the numbers in the phone.

__________________ 4. It's **unusually** for Jack to miss a class. He comes every day.

__________________ 5. The **approximation** number of people living in the United States is 307 million.

__________________ 6. For extra money, some students **delivery** newspapers every morning.

__________________ 7. I saw Julie **performance** in three cities.

Vocabulary Use

Vocabulary Note

Some of the target vocabulary in Chapter 1 has usages and meanings that are different from how they were used in the reading. To become a better reader, make sure you understand these phrase/usages:

code *a secret code, the honor code* (a set of rules of behavior)

draw *to draw conclusions, to draw a blank*

delivery *a delivery room, to deliver a speech*

True or False

Write T if the statement is true and F if the statement is false.

_____ 1. If you memorize something, you forget it easily.

_____ 2. Actors are performers, but truck drivers are not performers.

_____ 3. To use an ATM machine to get money, you need to have a code.

_____ 4. Pizza and babies are examples of things that are delivered.

_____ 5. It is unusual for it to snow in Florida.

Write about It

Read the statement. Write a paragraph stating if you agree or disagree. Try to give three reasons for your answer. Use at least three of the words from the chart on page 8.

Some performers such as movie stars and pop singers receive a huge amount of money for doing work that is not very important.

CHAPTER

2

Walking in the Air

Getting Ready to Read

Not all public performers actually perform on the street. Some of them perform above the street. One type of performer is a tightrope walker. Discuss these questions with a classmate.

1. Have you ever seen a performance by a tightrope walker? Where?
2. What types of skills does someone need to be able to do this?
3. Is it something you would like to try?

Vocabulary Preview

For each sentence, choose the word or phrase to match the meaning of the word in bold.

allowed by law	hanging
building	recognition
favorable	unlike anything else
focus	wish

1. The professor asked the students to give him their **attention.**

   I think **attention** means ______________________________.

2. It took the **construction** workers two years to build our new house.

   I think **construction** means ______________________________.

3. The United States received **credit** for putting the first human on the moon, but the U.S.S.R. had the honor of putting the first person in space.

   I think **credit** means ______________________________.

4. Many street performers have a **desire** to do something no one else has ever done. They want this experience very badly. Sometimes, they don't consider the risks.

   I think **desire** means ______________________________.

5. In many states, it isn't **legal** to drive a car and talk on a cell phone at the same time. If a police officer sees you using a cell phone while driving, the officer will give you a ticket.

   I think **legal** means ______________________________.

6. Is this glass half full or half empty? If you think that it is half full, you look at things in a **positive** way. If you think it is half empty, you look at things in a negative way.

   I think **positive** means ______________________________.

7. Hummingbirds look like they are **suspended** in air when they are feeding because their wings are moving too fast to see.

   I think **suspended** means ______________________________.

8. The view from the top of the mountain is **unique**. You can see the ocean miles away.

   I think **unique** means ____.

Reading Skill

Skill — **Scanning for Details**

Purpose — To find specific information quickly

Technique — When you scan, you look only for the information that you need. You move your eyes across the text to look only for the specific information. You don't read every word. Keep moving your eyes across the text until you find the information that you are looking for.

Example — *Questions*

1. When was the first law about street performing passed? (Look for dates to answer *when* questions.)
2. Who passed it? (Look for capital letters and names for answers to *who* questions.)

Passage

In 462 BCE, the Romans passed a law against street performing. If you sang a song about the government in public places, you could be put to death.

Scanning for Details

Scan the reading on pages 14–15 for the answers to these questions.

1. Where does Philippe Petit live? ______________________________
2. When did Philippe Petit walk between the towers? ____________________
3. How long was he walking there? ______________________________
4. How many times did he walk across the cable? ____________________

Reading

Walking in the Air: The Story of Philippe Petit

Philippe Petit is not like most people in the world. As a child, he was kicked out of five schools. He's been arrested* more than 500 times in several different countries. He was born in France, but he now lives in New York. He is building a barn by himself using only 18th century tools. All of these facts are true, but they are not what make Philippe Petit famous. He is famous for walking on a rope between the Twin Towers in New York City. As everyone knows, the Twin Towers are gone, but in 1974, they were new. Philippe drew worldwide **attention** to them by putting up a 450-pound cable** between them and walking on it for 45 minutes.

Philippe's **desire** to walk between the towers began six years earlier. He was a street performer and had walked on a tightrope many times. So, when he saw the towers being built, he wanted to walk between them. He spent those six years finding out more about the towers as they were being built. Since his plan wasn't **legal** and the towers had many locks, he had to first find ways of getting into the buildings. He dressed as a **construction** worker and a businessman. He hid under tarps*** and in elevators. He learned the codes to locks. He measured the wind speed and the distance between the towers. At home, he built models of the towers and practiced tightrope walking. He measured cables and gathered the equipment. Finally, on August 7, 1974, at 7:15 AM, he stepped out on the cable that was **suspended** between the towers.

---

*__arrested__—*v.* taken by the police

**__cable__—*n.* a thick rope

***__tarp__—*n.* a large piece of waterproof plastic used to cover things in the rain

Slowly, people began to notice that someone was walking between the two towers. Crowds gathered. Someone called the police. Philippe, however, was not concerned. He was having fun. He was getting a **unique** view of the towers. In all, he walked across the cable eight times. When he stepped off the cable, the police arrested him. However, they dropped the charges several days later. In fact, he was given a lifetime pass to the Observation Deck for the Twin Towers. He also received **credit** for bringing **positive** attention to the towers.

Now Philippe is more than 60 years old, but he still practices tightrope walking every day. And he is raising money for his next performance: walking on a cable across the Grand Canyon.

Reading Comprehension

Circle the letter of the correct answer, or write a short answer.

1. Why is Philippe Petit an unusual person?
   a. He was born in France, but he lives in New York.
   b. He walked on a rope between two towers in New York.
   c. He is more than 60 years old.
2. Philippe first worked at the towers before they were open to the public.
   a. true
   b. false
   c. The reading doesn't say.
3. Before 1974, Philippe had
   a. never walked on a tightrope.
   b. walked on a tightrope once or twice.
   c. walked on a tightrope many times.

4. When Philippe first stepped out on the wire, people on the street cheered for him.
   a. true
   b. false
   c. The reading doesn't say.

5. How many times did Philippe walk across the wire? ____________________

6. The police were not happy to see Philippe on the wire.
   a. true
   b. false
   c. The reading doesn't say.

7. After Philippe stepped off of the wire,
   a. the police arrested him.
   b. he spent three months in jail.
   c. both a and b

8. Philippe retired when he turned 60.
   a. true
   b. false
   c. The reading doesn't say.

Discuss Your Ideas

In small groups, discuss the answers to these questions. Be prepared to share your answers with the class.

1. Do you think that the police should have arrested Philippe? Why or why not?
2. Do you think you would like Philippe? Why or why not?
3. What do you think was the biggest risk that Philippe took? Why?
4. Why do you think people like Philippe take risks?
5. Do you take risks? In what ways?

STUDY TIP

Understanding How *You* Study

In order to be an effective student, you need to think about what you do when you study: what helps you study and what distracts you from studying? Answer the questions to get an understanding of how you study.

1. Where do you study? ______________________________
2. Do you study alone or with other students? ______________________
3. Do you need a quiet place, or can you study with noise around you? ______ ______________________________
4. When you read, do you take notes? ______________________
5. When you have to learn some vocabulary words or some facts for a test, how do you memorize them? ______________________
6. How can you change the way you study to make it better? __________ ______________________________

Vocabulary Comprehension

With a classmate, fill in the empty boxes in the chart. Do not write anything in the boxes that have an X. You can use an English dictionary.

Nouns	Verbs	Adjectives	Adverbs
attention	X		
construction		X	X
1. 2.	credit	X	X
desire			X
		legal	
X	X	positive	
	suspend	X	X
X	X	unique	

Sentence Completion

Fill in each blank with one of the words from the chart. Use the context to help you choose the correct form of the word.

1. The teacher didn't give me ______________ for my homework because I turned it in late. Next time, I have to turn it in on time so that she will know that I did it.
2. The ______________ for money can lead people to do things that they should not do.
3. I think that my son is going to be a ______________ worker. He loves to make buildings with small pieces of wood.
4. Each one of us is ______________ in our own way.
5. On German highways, cars can go as fast as the drivers want, but in most U.S. states, driving over 70 mph isn't ______________.
6. Are you ______________ that you can pick me up from the airport?
7. In my biology class, my professor is giving a lot of ______________ to the first chapter.
8. If you do something against the law, the police can ______________ your license.

Odd One Out

Circle the word that does not belong in each group. Be prepared to explain why the word does not belong.

1. build, construct, make, take
2. happy, helpful, positive, upset
3. attentive, careless, forgetful, sleepy
4. hang, land, stay in the air, suspend
5. legal, unfair, unlawful, wrong
6. normal, special, unique, unusual
7. acknowledgment, card, credit, recognition
8. desire, dislike, hate, not want

Vocabulary Use

Vocabulary Note

Some of the target vocabulary in Chapter 2 has usages and meanings that are different from how they were used in the reading. To become a better reader, make sure you understand these phrase/usages:

positive *to be positive* (sure, certain), *to test positive*

suspend *to suspend a license, to suspend production*

Short Answer

Write an answer to these questions. Try to use the word in bold in your answer.

1. Where is it **legal** to drive on the left side of the street? ____________________
2. What materials can be used to **construct** houses? ____________________
3. When should a driver be very **attentive**? ____________________

Write about It

Try to use at least three words from the chart on page 17.

It takes courage to perform in public. Are you the kind of person who would enjoy being a street performer? If so, what kind of performance would you give? If not, would you rather perform on stage or some other place? Write a paragraph describing the kind of performance you would like to give.

Vocabulary Skill

Skill	**Keeping a Vocabulary Journal**
Purpose	To learn vocabulary items in a systematic way
Technique	In a notebook, enter the targeted vocabulary words for each chapter. Each word gets one page (front and back). 1. On the front of each page, write all the forms of the word. 2. On the back, write a brief definition <u>or</u> translation, the pronunciation, and sample sentence or phrase. If you have seen the word used in different ways (noun and verb) or have different meaning, add a definition for each. 3. If you like, you can also write the translation in your native language.
Example	

Front	Back
amazement, n. amaze, v. amazing, adj. amazingly, adv.	a big surprise [ah-māy-z-ment] I saw the <u>amazement</u> on the child's face when he saw his new bicycle.

Keeping a Vocabulary Log

Start your own Vocabulary Journal. Write entries for words from Unit 1.

1. approximately
2. delivery
3. performance

Timed Reading

Read the passage according to your teacher's instructions. Then answer the questions on page 209 without looking at the reading.

The Hip Hop Phenomenon

Hip hop is a unique part of urban culture in the United States. It began in the 1970s in a neighborhood of New York City called the Bronx. At that time, the Bronx was full of poverty, unemployment, and hopelessness. Young people especially felt restless and depressed. But amazingly, out of this disorder, an original and significant music and dance movement began. It happened when young men and women gathered on street corners and tried to forget their troubles by playing music and dancing.

The music of hip hop is called rap. Rap originated with the Jamaican immigrants in New York City. They brought some techniques of reggae music with them and adapted them to rap. For example, one Jamaican immigrant, Kool Herc, used the idea of "toasting" from reggae music. In reggae, "toasting" is talking over parts of songs, so Kool Herc began to talk in rhymes to the beat of hip hop music. Another original development in hip hop is the DJ. DJs are disc jockeys that use records and turntables to create unique blends of music and song.

The dance style of hip hop music is called break dancing. Break dancing styles developed to the familiar rhythms of African music and the poetry of rappers. It is a combination of recognized movements and individual variations. Typical break dance moves are Toprock and Downrock. As their names indicate, Toprock dancing uses the top half of the body, and Downrock is movement of the feet. The "moon walk," which was made famous by Michael Jackson, is a Downrock move. Break dance Power Moves require a lot of skill

and strength. In Windmill, for example, dancers support their weight on one hand and then move their bodies in different ways in the air. In Headspin,
* dancers spin upside down with their heads on the sidewalk while their bodies move above them to the beat of the music. These moves look random and unplanned, but becoming a good hip hop dancer requires skill, strength, and a lot of practice.

From the streets of the Bronx, hip hop fans followed their favorite rappers and DJs into nightclubs. Smart record company executives offered recording contracts to popular rappers. Their CDs sold millions of copies. Hip hop dancers began to perform on the streets and in clubs worldwide. In just a few short years, hip hop became an essential part of American culture.

UNIT 2

Traveling on Foot

Walking is one of the most common things people do. It is the usual way people get from one place to another without a form of transportation, such as a car or bicycle. Most people walk at least a little bit each day. Even so, it seems that people don't walk as much as they used to.

Answer these questions with a partner.

1. What are some reasons people walk in daily life?
2. Why are some reasons people might walk long distances for travel or special occasions?
3. Why do you think people don't walk as much as they used to?
4. What health benefits can be gained from walking?
5. Are you a walker? How often do you walk? How far do you walk? How do you decide when to walk and when to take a form of transportation?

CHAPTER 3

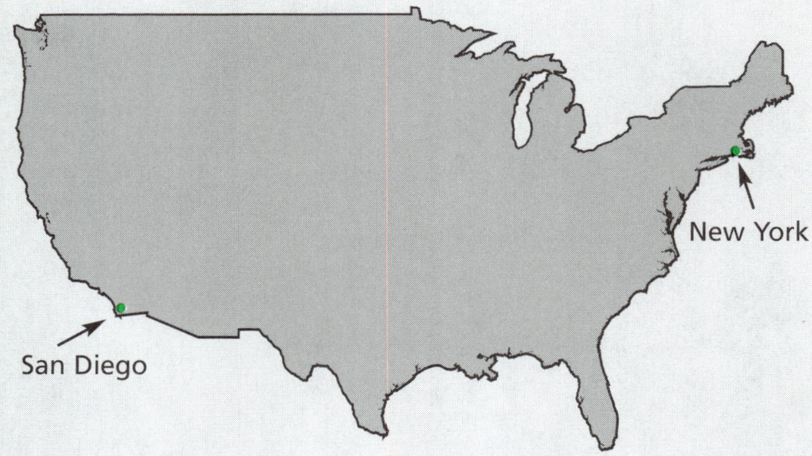

Fat Man Walking

Getting Ready to Read

Look at the map. Discuss these questions.

1. How long do you think it takes to walk from San Diego to New York?
2. Can you think of any reasons to walk across the United States?
3. What is the longest distance that you have ever walked?

Vocabulary Preview

For each sentence, choose one of the words or phrases to match the meaning of the word in bold.

extra
feel sorry
not selfish, giving
physical heaviness
refuse or say no
sadness
being very overweight
way of seeing, point of view

1. You're sitting at home all day, thinking about your problems. The doctor said it was called **depression.**

   I think **depression** means ______________________________.

2. It's easy to gain **weight** if you eat more food than you need. Your body will turn **excess** food into fat.

   I think **weight** means ______________________________.

   I think **excess** means ______________________________.

3. Doctors explain that **obesity** means having more fat than is healthy.

   I think **obesity** means ______________________________.

4. My aunt is a very **generous** woman. She always shares food with her neighbors and takes time to help them whenever they need help.

   I think **generous** means ______________________________

5. Traveling to poor countries really changed my **perspective** on food. I used to waste food, but now I realize that many people don't have enough food to eat.

   I think **perspective** means ______________________________.

6. I **regret** spending money on new clothes. Now I don't have enough money to fix my car.

   I think **regret** means ______________________________.

7. My sister is trying to stay in good shape. When we go to a restaurant, she **resists** the dessert and just orders coffee instead.

   I think **resist** means ______________________________.

Reading Skill

Skill	**Skimming for the Main Idea**
Purpose	To find the main ideas quickly.
Explanation	Skimming is used to understand the general main idea of a passage by reading it quickly without stopping to look up the meaning of individual words. Skimming is also used to see if you are interested in a text and want to read it more carefully.
Examples	Some examples of skimming include: 1. reading the headlines in a newspaper or on a news website quickly to learn the general news of the day 2. looking at the titles of several articles in a magazine to decide which ones you want to read more carefully
Technique	Skimming is much faster than word-by-word reading. When you skim, move your eyes over the page or the screen three to four times more quickly than usual. When you skim, read the first and last paragraphs as well as the first sentence of each paragraph. This will give you a general idea of how a reading passage is organized and what topics are included. Remember, you are only looking for information to help you understand the reading. You are also deciding whether you want to read the passage more carefully.

Skimming for the Main Idea

Skim the reading to find the main idea of each paragraph. Write the paragraph number next to each main idea.

____ Steve met generous strangers on the road and even went on TV at the end of his 13-month journey.

____ Steve hasn't given up and is planning another journey on foot.

____ Steve decided to walk across the country for two reasons.

____ Steve's writing on the Internet about his journey attracted attention.

____ Steve inspired other people, but he wasn't able to help himself.

Reading

Fat Man Walking

(1) Steve Vaught was a young man living in San Diego, California. In 1990, his life changed forever when he killed two pedestrians* in a car accident. After this, he became very **depressed**. He turned to **excess** food for comfort, and his **weight** increased to approximately 400 pounds. In 2005, he decided to walk across the entire** United States—from San Diego to New York. By crossing the country on foot, he not only hoped to lose the **excess weight,** but he also hoped to gain a more positive **perspective** on his life.

(2) Vaught used the Internet to record his journey across the United States. On his website (fatmanwalking.com), he described his adventures and explored his thoughts on **obesity** and **depression**. He soon attracted the attention of journalists and filmmakers. Some walked beside him on the roads of America for a while.

(3) As he crossed the country, Vaught slept in a tent or stayed in the homes of **generous** strangers who had learned about his journey and wanted to show their support. After 13 months, he finally reached New York. In New York, he rode in a limousine, slept in a luxury hotel, and appeared on major television shows. On these shows, he described his trip as being very lonely at times. At other times, however, he said he enjoyed being alone in quiet places where he found a sense of peace.

***pedestrians**—*pl. n.* walkers

****entire**—*adj.* complete, whole

(4) As his journey became widely known in news articles and on the Internet, Vaught had the chance to inspire others who wanted to change their lives in a positive way. Unfortunately, some of the changes in Vaught's life have not been so positive. Vaught is no longer married, and the "fat man" has been unable to reach a normal **weight**, despite his trek*** of 3,000 miles.

(5) After the trek, Vaught lived in a hotel room in San Diego. He is still trying to reduce his size by following a sensible diet. (On the road, it was difficult for him to **resist** the American fast food that he found in each city and town.) In the end, Vaught does not regret the time he spent traveling across the United States on foot. He has announced new plans to walk around the world, leaving San Diego and traveling again on the road. The fat man will still be walking—next time in different places, but with the same goal of improving his life and health.

***__trek__—*n.* a long trip

Reading Comprehension

Circle the letter of the correct answer, or write a short answer.

1. Films were made, and stories were written about Steve Vaught.
   a. true
   b. false
   c. The reading doesn't say.
2. Where did Vaught stay during his journey across the United States?

   ____

3. Which of the following did he NOT do in New York?
   a. ride in a limousine
   b. appear on TV
   c. meet the mayor

4. What was positive and negative about walking alone for Steve? ____________

____

5. Vaught's trek encouraged other people to do positive things.
   a. true
   b. false
   c. The reading doesn't say.
6. Walking 3,000 miles helped Vaught reach a normal weight.
   a. true
   b. false
   c. The reading doesn't say.
7. What does Vaught plan to do next? ____________________

Discuss Your Ideas

In small groups, discuss the answers to these questions. Be prepared to share your answers with the class.

1. Do you think it was a good idea for Vaught to walk across the United States? Why or why not?
2. Do you think walking a long distance can change your perspective on your life? Why or why not?
3. How long do you think it takes to walk across other countries?

STUDY TIP

Using the Internet: Finding Maps

Maps can be very helpful when you read about cities and countries of the world. To find a map of New York City, for example, type "map of New York City" in your search engine. You will have several choices to click on and look at more closely. Looking at a map of a place before you read about it will help improve your reading comprehension.

Vocabulary Comprehension

Fill in the empty boxes in the chart. Do not write anything in the boxes that have an X. You can use an English dictionary.

Nouns	Verbs	Adjectives	Adverbs
depression	X	1. 2.	X
	X	1. excess 2.	
	X	generous	
obesity	X		X
perspective	X	X	X
regret			
	resist		X
weight			

Matching

Match each word in the left column with its opposite meaning in the right column.

____ 1. depression	a. feeling of satisfaction about something
____ 2. excessive	b. lightness
____ 3. generosity	c. weak
____ 4. regret	d. not enough
____ 5. resistant	e. happiness
____ 6. weight	f. selfishness

Word Forms

Read the sentences. Change the incorrect word form in bold to the correct form.

__________________ 1. You will gain weight if you eat an **excessively** amount of food.

__________________ 2. **Generosity** people will share their food with others.

__________________ 3. **Obese** is becoming a health problem around the world.

__________________ 4. I **regrettable** that I ate so much last night.

__________________ 5. I cannot **resistance** delicious foods like chocolate cake.

__________________ 6. Do you know how much you **weight**?

Vocabulary Use

Vocabulary Note

Some of the target vocabulary in Chapter 3 has usages and meanings that are different from how they were used in the reading. To become a better reader, make sure you understand these phrase/usages:

excess/excessive *excess food* (used with a noun) but *an excessive amount of food* (used with the expressions *amount of* or *quantity of*)

resistance *the path of least resistance, a resistance to sickness*

weigh *to weigh on someone's mind*

True or False

Write T if the statement is true and F if the statement is false.

____ 1. People who live in cold climates need to wear an excessive amount of clothing.

____ 2. You may lose friends if you act generously.

____ 3. Too much exercise can cause obesity.

____ 4. Our perspective on our life can change as we grow older.

____ 5. We often regret doing things that make us unhappy.

____ 6. You won't have enough shoes if you can't resist shoe shopping.

____ 7. Our weight depends only on how much healthy food we eat.

Write about It

Read the statement. Write a paragraph in response to the topic. Try to use three words from the chart on page 30.

Obesity is a serious problem in many countries of the world, but especially in the United States. What are the main causes of obesity? How can being obese affect someone's life?

CHAPTER

4

Travelogues

"A traveler without observation is a bird without wings."

This quote is from the writings of a beloved Iranian poet, Muslihuddin Sadi (1184–1291). Sadi spent his life traveling throughout the Middle East and talking to people about their customs, beliefs, and dreams. It is through his writings about his journeys that we can understand life at that time and place.

The quote also explains why travelogues are still such a popular style of writing. At their best, travelogues allow readers to experience unknown places and people. The best travelogue writers are good observers of their surroundings and of life experiences.

Getting Ready to Read

With a classmate, discuss these questions. Be prepared to share your thoughts with the class.

1. What do Sadi's words mean? Do you agree with them? Why or why not?
2. Have you travelled much? Have you written about your travels? Have you ever read a travelogue?
3. What are some places and people that you are interested in? Where would you like to travel?

Vocabulary Preview

For each sentence, choose one of the words or phrases to match the meaning of the word in bold.

get	piled up
looking for	rest
a machine for transportation	told about a risk or danger
make something necessary	very much, a lot

1. When my mother went on vacation to Europe, her newspapers and mail **accumulated.**

   I think **accumulated** means ______________________________.

2. Raising children can be difficult at times, but all parents say that they **derive** great pleasure from watching their children grow into adults.

   I think **derive** means ______________________________.

3. We have to find sources of power that are renewable and therefore limitless. Using renewable sources is **infinitely** better than using non-renewable sources because they don't cause as much pollution.

   I think **infinitely** means ____.

4. Many years ago, weekends were times for families to **relax** at home, but today family members are busy doing many things away from home.

   I think **relax** means ____.

5. After weeks of **seeking** a job, I finally found one that I wanted. I start my new job next Monday.

   I think **seeking** means ____.

6. The top universities **require** high scores on certain tests before they accept students.

   I think **require** means ____.

7. My husband and I drive very different **vehicles**. He drives a huge truck, and I drive a small car.

   I think **vehicles** means ____.

8. George **warned** me that the hike would be very difficult. I thought I was in good condition, but I was wrong. I had to stop before the end.

   I think **warned** means ____.

Reading Skill

Skill	**Understanding Metaphors and Similes**
Purpose	To increase your ability to understand descriptions
Explanation	Metaphors and similes are comparisons between two things or ideas that usually aren't comparable or similar at all. They are used to describe something in a way that is interesting and/or beautiful. A metaphor is a direct comparison. A simile uses *like* or *as* to make the comparison.
Example	1. **The trees on the mountainside were graceful dancers in the wind. (metaphor)** 2. **The trees on the mountainside moved like dancers on stage. (simile)**
Technique	In these examples, the author is comparing the movement of the trees to dancing. By doing this, the author wants the reader to experience the same feeling. Readers may not have ever been on a mountainside, but they can still feel what it is like.

Defining Metaphors and Similes

Work with a classmate. Look at each underlined metaphor or simile. Rewrite the metaphor or simile. Use a dictionary if necessary.

1. Then lightning crashed like cymbals and a rain of what sounded like violas and cellos and whistling flutes enveloped me. ______________________________

   ____

2. We were greeted by a priest who led us into the statue of the saint that crowns the altar. ______________________________

   ____

3. "The road and her energy will provide all you need," Anna told me. ____________

   ____

4. She told me I would find a stick to walk with. It would speak to me as though it would want to help. ______________________________

   ____

Reading

Excerpts from

The Camino: A Journey of the Spirit

By Shirley MacLaine

(1) There is a famous pilgrimage[*] that has been taken by people for centuries called the Santiago de Compostela Camino across northern Spain. It is said that the "Camino"—the road or the way—lies directly under the Milky Way and follows ley lines[**] that reflect the energy from those star systems above it. . . .

The Path of El Camino through Spain

(2) The Camino, following the earth's ley lines, begins in France, crosses the Pyrenees, and makes its way from east to west across northern Spain until it reaches an exquisite[***] and very famous cathedral called Santiago de Compostela, where the remains[†] of Saint James are said to be interred.[††]

(3) I have never been religious, opting instead to **seek** spirituality, so what interested me about the Camino was the energy of the ley lines themselves, as well as the challenge of walking alone for 800 kilometers (nearly 500 miles) and becoming essentially helpless and vulnerable[†††] along the way, as most pilgrimages **require**.

. . .

[*]**pilgrimage**—*n.* a spiritual or religious journey
[**]**ley lines**—*pl. n.* according to some people, invisible lines that exist on the earth and have a lot of energy around them
[***]**exquisite**—*adj.* very beautiful
[†]**remains**—*pl. n.* a dead body
[††]**interred**—*v.* buried
[†††]**vulnerable**—*adj.* unprotected

(4) Whenever I travel, I prefer to do it light; however, seven pounds of lightness was new to me. Having done the trek herself, my Brazilian friend Anna Strong **warned** me that each ounce I carried in my backpack would become tons after a few weeks. . . .

(5) I am a Taurus,‡ and therefore a person who **accumulates** things. I immediately understood this journey would be an examination of what was essential to me. "The road and her energy will provide all you need," Anna told me. She told me I would find a stick to walk with. It would speak to me as though it would want to help. My feet would **derive** energy from the road itself, which is why it is **infinitely** better to walk than to ride the Camino in a **vehicle**.

. . .

(6) The next day was entirely different. Each village blurred into the next. I was somewhere in the state of Palencia. I walked alone again.

(7) Slowly the pain left my legs and feet. My shoulders **relaxed**, and I actually started to skip. . . .

(8) The trees on the mountainside seemed to be dancing to the music of the wind. It was my favorite kind of orchestral‡‡ performance. A storm cloud would thunder a percussion. Then lightning crashed like cymbals and a rain of what sounded like violas and cellos and whistling flutes enveloped me.

(9) I was utterly happy and part of everything around me.

. . .

(10) I felt I was somehow walking west to the end of the world. And then I wondered: Was I walking toward the beginning of the world as we now know it? Would I finish the Camino where it all began? And what place would that be? The edge of the "known world," they said, was where the Camino finished—Finesterre. What had finished? Was there a world that had somehow finished?

. . .

‡**Taurus**—*n.* according to the Zodiac, someone who was born between April 20 and May 20
‡‡**orchestral**—*adj.* being part of an orchestra or group of musicians

(11) And at last, we reached the magnificent cathedral in Compostela and climbed the stone stairway. Begun in the ninth century, it is an architectural marvel, a masterpiece that houses the tomb of Saint James beneath its high altar.‡‡‡

(12) We were greeted by a priest who led us into the statue of the saint that crowns the altar. As was customary, I climbed the stairs, which were behind the statue, and stood there looking up at the back of its head. Anna took a picture of me hugging the statue. I gave Saint James my thanks for being an inspiration to do this journey.

‡‡‡**altar**—*n.* a raised area at the front of a church

Reading Comprehension

Circle the letter of the correct answer, or write a short answer.

1. What is the "Camino?" ______________________________

2. According to MacLaine, there are many ley lines on the earth.
   a. true
   b. false
   c. The reading doesn't say.

3. According to MacLaine, why are ley lines important?
   a. They reflect the energy of outer space.
   b. They are a religious symbol of energy.
   c. Both a and b

4. Normally, MacLaine's luggage weighs more than seven pounds.
   a. true
   b. false
   c. The reading doesn't say.

5. Why is the cathedral Santiago de Compostela famous?
    a. It is the edge of the known world.
    b. People start their pilgrimages there.
    c. It may contain the body of Saint James.
6. What were the challenges of the Camino for MacLaine?
    a. to test her ability to walk alone for many days
    b. to discover what possessions of hers were absolutely necessary
    c. Both a and b
7. MacLaine's friend Anna told her to bring a walking stick.
    a. true
    b. false
    c. The reading doesn't say.
8. In Paragraph 8, MacLaine compares a storm to
    a. dancing
    b. a piece of music
    c. whistling
9. How does the storm make MacLaine feel? ______________________________
10. MacLaine was able to hug the statue of Saint James when she finally arrived at the cathedral.
    a. true
    b. false
    c. The reading doesn't say.

Discuss Your Ideas

In small groups, discuss the answers to these questions. Be prepared to share your answers with the class.

1. Do you know about any other pilgrimage routes? Where are they?
2. Have you or anyone you know ever been on a pilgrimage like this? If so, explain the journey to your classmates. If not, do you think you would like to go on one? Why or why not?
3. Read Paragraph 10 again. Why do you think MacLaine wrote this paragraph? What was she feeling at the time?
4. How do you think MacLaine felt when she finally reached Compostela?

STUDY TIP

Understanding Ellipsis Marks

Writers use ellipsis marks when they want to copy a passage from another writer but don't want to use the whole passage. As a reader, when you see ellipses, you know that something from the original passage has been omitted or left out. Usually, this means that the missing part of the passage is not critical to the point that the author wants to make. For example, there are ellipses marks between Paragraphs 3 and 4. This means that the writer omitted one or more sentences for the purposes of his or her writing. Be careful when using ellipses in writing up research. Your English handbook can provide more guidelines for using ellipses in academic writing.

Vocabulary Comprehension

With a classmate, fill in the empty boxes in the chart. Do not write anything in the boxes that have an X. You can use an English dictionary.

Nouns	Verbs	Adjectives	Adverbs
	accumulate		X
1. 2.	derive		X
X		infinitely	
relax		X	
require	X		X
	seek	X	X
vehicle	X		X
	warn	X	X

Sentence Completion

Fill in each blank with one of the words from the chart. Use the context to help you choose the correct form of the word.

1. Most people who go on pilgrimages ______________ something even though they may not know what it is.
2. Did you hear the fire alarm? That's a ______________ that we should get out of the building.
3. In order to graduate from the university, you must fulfill many ______________. You have to pass general education classes and classes for your major.
4. Gardening is a ______________ hobby for me. I enjoy being outside, digging in the dirt, and planting flowers. I also ______________ a lot of pleasure from watching my flowers grow and bloom.
5. Jose will only ride in a ______________ with airbags. In case of an accident, he wants an airbag to protect him.

6. The number of stars in the universe is ______________.

7. Many college students borrow money to pay for college and ______________ a lot of debt.

Odd One Out

Circle the word that does not belong in each group. Be prepared to explain why the word does not belong.

1. calm down, jog, relax, rest
2. accumulate, add to, gather, throw away
3. car, bicycle, motorcycle, vehicle
4. discover, find, locate, seek
5. derive, end, remove, take away
6. inform, notify, tell, warn
7. desire, must have, need, require
8. a little, infinite, not much, a small amount

Vocabulary Use

Vocabulary Note

Some of the target vocabulary in Chapter 4 has usages and meanings that are different from how they were used in the reading. To become a better reader, make sure you understand these phrase/usages:

derive *to derive pleasure, a derivation* (the origin of something)

Short Answer

Write an answer to these questions. Try to use the word in bold in your answer.

1. What kind of **vehicle** does a hospital need? ______________________________

2. How do you **accumulate** enough money to buy a house? ____________________

3. Whom does a child **derive** the most comfort from at home? _________________

4. Where can you **seek** shelter in the rain? ______________________________

Write about It

Look at the figure. Write a paragraph in response to this prompt. Try to use three words from the chart on page 42.

Shirley MacLaine mentions that her astrological sign is Taurus. Do you know your own astrological sign? How strong is your belief in astrology—the idea that our time of birth and the placement of stars influence our lives?

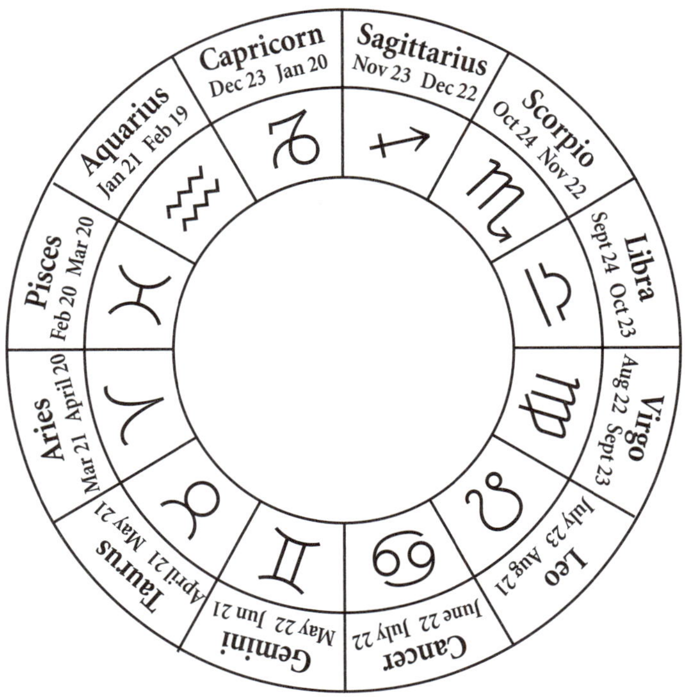

Vocabulary Skill

Skill	**Understanding Word Forms: Nouns, Verbs, Adjectives, and Adverbs**
Purpose	To be better able to understand word relationships in sentences
Explanation	**Nouns** These are words for people, places, things, or ideas. For example, *child, school, hat,* and *love* are all nouns. **Verbs** There are two kinds of verbs: action verbs and non-action verbs. **Action verbs,** such as *walk, eat,* and *sleep,* describe physical actions. **Non-action verbs** include *be* and *become*; they also include words of emotion (*hate, love*) and words that describe mental states (*know, understand*). **Adjectives** These words give more information about nouns. For example, *blue, windy, wild,* and *important* are adjectives. **Adverbs** These words give us more information about verbs, adjectives, and other adverbs. You can usually make adverbs by adding *–ly* to adjectives. Be careful because sometimes adjectives and adverbs are the same. For example, the words *fast, hard, early,* and *late* can be both adjectives and adverbs.

Word Forms

Read each word and decide its part of speech. Write N for noun, AV for action verb, NV for non-action verb, ADJ for adjective, or ADV for adverb. Some words could have more than one answer.

____	1. agree	____	6. city	____	11. know	____	16. say
____	2. banana	____	7. eye	____	12. kiss	____	17. smile
____	3. belong	____	8. fast	____	13. news	____	18. sweetly
____	4. brother	____	9. happy	____	14. pretty	____	19. truth
____	5. Charlie	____	10. bright	____	15. quickly	____	20. yellow

Timed Reading

Read the passage according to your teacher's instructions. Then answer the questions on page 210 without looking at the reading.

The Triple Crown of Hiking

For serious hikers, the United States offers the Triple Crown of Hiking. The Triple Crown has three north-south trails that go through the major mountain ranges: the Appalachians in the east, the Sierra Nevada and Cascade Range in the west, and the Rocky Mountains in the middle of the country.

The oldest of these established trails is the Appalachian Trail, which runs through the Appalachian Mountains from Maine to Georgia. In total, it covers fourteen states and 2,160 miles. Only about 10,000 hikers have hiked the entire length of the trail in one year. These one-season hikes are called thru-
* hikes and can take four to six months to complete. Most thru-hikers start in Georgia in March or April and hike north. By doing this, they do not have to hike through the snow in the northern mountains.

The Pacific Crest Trail is about 500 miles longer than the Appalachian Trail and covers a greater variety of eco-zones—from the mountain cold in the Sierra Nevada to the desert heat in Southern California. It goes from just north of Mexico near San Diego to just across the border in British Columbia,
* Canada. In order to cover at least twenty miles a day, thru-hikers travel light. In fact, as part of the planning, hikers may send themselves packages at various post offices along the way. They also have to determine where they can buy supplies.

The last trail of the Triple Crown, the Continental Divide Trail in the middle of the country, is the newest, the least charted and the longest at 3,100 miles. The trail stays as much as possible on the Continental Divide, which it

the line that determines which way—east or west—water flows. It is probably the most difficult trail to thru-hike. The section in Colorado averages about
* 11,000 feet in altitude, so hikers must travel through snow. Also, some hikers get altitude sickness, which may slow them down or cause serious health risks. In addition, there are parts of this trail in New Mexico that have not been charted, so the hikers also need to navigate the trail. A compass and a map are essential on all trails but particularly on the Continental Divide Trail.

While thru-hiking on any of the three Triple Crown Trails takes time, money and incredible strength, all provide spectacular views, unmatched adventure, and a real sense of the beautiful lands of the United States.

UNIT 3

The Ends of the Earth

Some places are described as "the ends of the earth." This means they are very far away from people and other places.

Answer these questions with a partner.

1. Would you like to visit or live in a place like this? Why or why not?
2. How would you spend your time if there were no people around and no modern items, like refrigerators or televisions?
3. Can you name any places that are at the ends of the earth? Where are they? What have you heard about them?
4. Type each location in the left column into an Internet search engine. Match it to the closest and more well-known location.

1. Luangwa Valley	a. Africa
2. Pilbara	b. Alaska
3. Ross Island	c. Antarctica
4. Gulu Village	d. Australia
5. St. Matthew Island	e. China

CHAPTER 5

My Bookworm Blog

Getting Ready to Read

Read this quotation by American author, Henry David Thoreau (1816–1862):

> *"A man is rich in proportion to the number of things he can afford to let alone."*

Choose the sentence that best explains the quotation.

a. Being rich depends on not needing much.

b. Being rich depends on buying many things.

c. Being rich depends on being able to afford things.

Discuss these questions with a partner.

1. How much money do you need to feel happy?
2. What are some things (besides money) that make you happy?
3. Do you think you could live by yourself without a car, a computer, nice clothes, or delicious food? Explain your answer.
4. Do you enjoy spending time outdoors? Why or why not?

Vocabulary Preview

For each sentence, choose one of the words or phrases to match the meaning of the word in bold.

bad use of something	opinion
dependent on oneself	a place to live
an exciting experience	stay alive
making bad decisions	think something is special

1. Many people **admire** the U.S. author Henry David Thoreau for his philosophy of life, which he expressed in his essays.

   I think **admire** means ______________________________.

2. When I read Thoreau's book, my **impression** was that he understood government, health, and nature.

   I think **impression** means ______________________________.

3. Thoreau was interested in how people can find a way to **survive** by themselves in bad weather and difficult situations.

   I think **survive** means ______________________________.

4. Thoreau also wrote that humans and animals will do anything for food to eat and for **shelter** to keep themselves warm and dry.

   I think **shelter** means ______________________________.

5. Living alone in a forest is an **adventure.** You need to be strong, brave, and prepared for unexpected things.

   I think **adventure** means ______________________________.

6. Some people **waste** food instead of saving it for later.

   I think **waste** means ______________________________.

7. My brother is a very **self-reliant** person. I never have to help him with anything. Sometimes I never even know he has a problem.

   I think **self-reliant** means ______________________________________.

8. He was **foolish** to reject the teacher's offer of help.

   I think **foolish** means ______________________________________.

Reading Skill

Skill	**Deciding When to Use a Dictionary**
Purpose	To help you choose the words you need to look up in a dictionary
Explanation	Looking up all the words you don't know will slow down your reading and make it harder for you to understand what you are reading. Reading well involves more than understanding the meaning of individual words. Reading well involves understanding the ideas of the entire text. You don't need to know the meaning of every single word in order to understand the main ideas. Follow the steps in the diagram on page 53 to decrease the number of times you have to stop your reading to look in a dictionary. To start, you should read the entire page at least one time before looking up words in a dictionary.

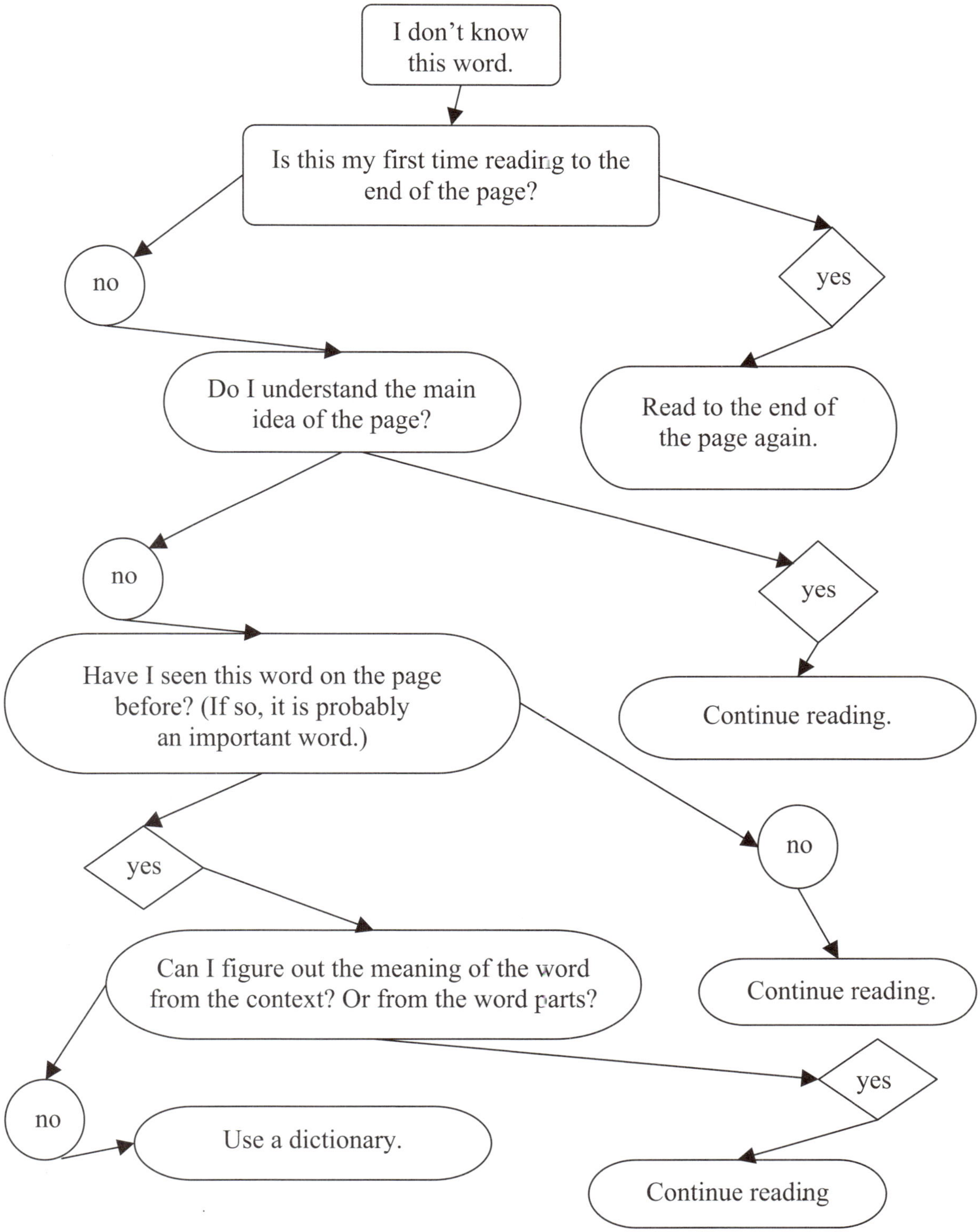
I don't know this word.
Is this my first time reading to the end of the page?
no
yes
Read to the end of the page again.
Do I understand the main idea of the page?
no
yes
Continue reading.
Have I seen this word on the page before? (If so, it is probably an important word.)
yes
no
Continue reading.
Can I figure out the meaning of the word from the context? Or from the word parts?
no
Use a dictionary.
yes
Continue reading

Deciding When to Use a Dictionary

Several words are underlined in these two paragraphs. With a classmate, decide which word you would look up in a dictionary. You can only choose one word from each paragraph. Be prepared to share your selection with the class.

1. I have mixed feelings about the book's protagonist, Christopher McCandless. On one hand, I admire him. He was a kind young man who loved nature and believed in adventure. On the other hand, he made such mind-boggling mistakes. Sometimes I think that he squandered his life and broke the hearts of the people who loved him.

2. McCandless found an old school bus, which he used as refuge. He hunted small animals and also survived by ingesting plants. Three months later, he decided to leave his refuge and return to other people. But he was unable to cross the Teklanika River. Lacking a map, he didn't know that he was very close to an easy way to cross the river safely. So McCandless returned to his refuge and continued hunting for food. He possibly ate some plants that made him sick. He became weak and scrawny.

3. Jim Gallien was the last person who saw McCandless in Alaska. Gallien gave him a lift from Fairbanks to the Stampede Trail. He was impressed by McCandless' intelligence and comportment. But he didn't think that McCandless was carrying enough food and gear. Gallien wanted to drive him to Anchorage, where he could buy more equipment, but McCandless wasn't interested. Finally, the young man acquiesced to take a few things from Gallien: a pair of boots, a couple of tuna sandwiches, and a bag of corn chips. That's all he wanted as he began his perilous trek into Alaska, alone.

Reading

This reading comes from an Internet blog. This style of writing is usually personal and informal. "My Bookworm Blog" is written by a person who loves to read books and to share his opinions about them online.

Into the Wild by Jon Krakauer

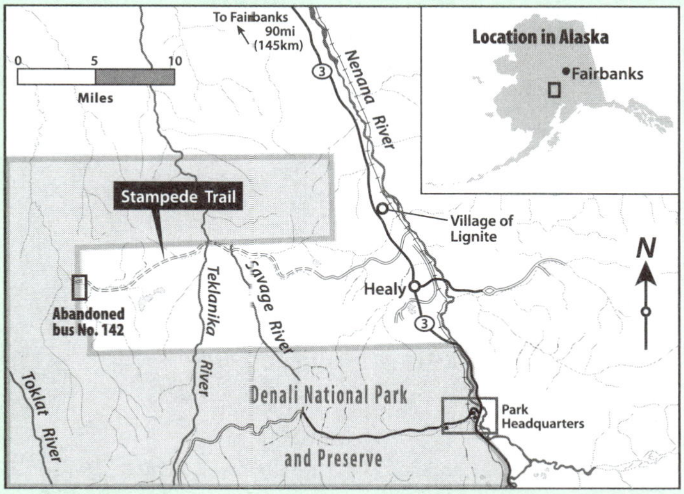

I love books about **adventure,** so I really enjoyed *Into the Wild* by Jon Krakauer. But now I have mixed feelings about the book's subject, Christopher McCandless. On one hand, I **admire** him. He was a kind young man who loved nature and believed in adventure. On the other hand, he made such unbelievable mistakes. Sometimes I think that he **wasted** his life and broke the hearts of the people who loved him.

McCandless grew up in very nice town on the East Coast. In high school, he loved running and told his running teammates to run away from all the "darkness" and bad things in the world. After college, he gave his remaining school money—$27,000—to charity.* Then, he started traveling through the western United States. He didn't care about having a good job or buying a nice house. He wanted to enjoy nature and live a **self-reliant** life. He didn't want to depend on a job, a credit card, or a shopping mall. Like one of his favorite authors, Henry David Thoreau, he wanted to live a simple life in nature.

***charity**—*n.* an organization that helps people, usually people who need money or food

Jim Gallien was the last person who saw the young adventurer in Alaska. He gave McCandless a ride from Fairbanks to the Stampede Trail. McCandless' intelligence and good manners made an **impression** on him. But he didn't think that McCandless was carrying enough food and equipment. Gallien wanted to drive him to Anchorage, where he could buy more equipment, but McCandless wasn't interested. Finally, the young man agreed to take a few things from Gallien: a pair of boots, a couple of tuna sandwiches, and a bag of corn chips. That's all he wanted as he began his dangerous trek into Alaska, alone.

We know the rest of the story from reading McCandless' journal. He found an old school bus, which he used as **shelter.** He hunted small animals and also **survived** by eating plants. But he had no map or compass,** which is something I still don't understand. Three months later, he decided to leave the school bus and return to other people. But he was unable to cross the Teklanika River. Without a map, he didn't know that he was very close to an easy way to cross the river safely. McCandless returned to the bus and continued hunting for food. He possibly ate some plants that made him sick. He became weaker and weaker. In about one month, he died after writing these words in his journal: "I have had a happy life, thank the Lord. May God bless all."

Into the Wild is one of the most interesting books that I have read this year. Like many true stories, Into The Wild has become a movie. I plan to see it soon. I'm sure it will be exciting, but I don't think it will answer my question about Christopher McCandless. Who was he—a man of freedom or a **fool**?

****compass**—*n.* a device that shows direction (north, south, east, west)

Reading Comprehension

Circle the letter of the correct answer, or write a short answer.

1. Which phrase best describes the blog author's attitude toward McCandless?
   a. completely positive
   b. completely negative
   c. both positive and negative
2. What guess can we make about McCandless from Paragraph 1?
   a. He enjoyed being outdoors.
   b. He had unbelievable adventures with friends.
   c. He was admired by many others.
3. According to the blog, McCandless spent all his money on a college education.
   a. true
   b. false
   c. The reading doesn't say.
4. According to the blog, what was McCandless' main reason for traveling through the western United States?
   a. to take a break from working
   b. to raise money for charity
   c. to live simply without many things
5. Which phrase best describes Jim Gallien?
   a. a close friend who cared about McCandless
   b. a stranger who helped McCandless
   c. an adventurer who traveled with McCandless
6. According to the blog, Gallien drove McCandless to Anchorage to buy more equipment.
   a. true
   b. false
   c. The reading doesn't say.

7. What can we guess from the blog about what McCandless cared about most?
   a. writing
   b. reading
   c. nature

8. According to the blog, what was one of McCandless' mistakes?
   a. using a bus for shelter
   b. not bringing a map
   c. eating small animals

9. According to the blog, which phrase best describes McCandless' attitude at the end of his life?
   a. frightened and angry
   b. unemotional
   c. thankful and positive

10. The blog author is still unsure about his opinion of McCandless.
    a. true
    b. false
    c. The reading doesn't say.

Discuss Your Ideas

In small groups, discuss the answers to these questions. Be prepared to share your answers with the class.

1. Do you enjoy reading adventure stories? What other adventure stories have you read?
2. McCandless was influenced by the writings of Thoreau. What book or author has influenced you?
3. Why do you think McCandless wrote a journal during his time alone in Alaska? How do you think it helped him?
4. Would you consider living or traveling alone in nature? Why or why not?

STUDY TIP

Managing Your Study Space

Many educators tell students to find one place to study and to make that place their own. Some students find that they can study well in a quiet library, others do better in a busy coffee shop. Still others prefer to study at home. However, recent research has shown that changing the study place may actually help students remember information. When you look for places to study, consider the lighting, music (or silence), and convenience of each place. In each space, make sure that you have everything you need to study so that you can focus on the material.

Vocabulary Comprehension

With a classmate, fill in the empty boxes in the chart. Do not write anything in the boxes that have an X. You can use an English dictionary.

Nouns	Verbs	Adjectives	Adverbs
	admire		
1. adventure 2.	X		X
fool			
		1. impressed 2.	
	X	self-reliant	X
shelter			X
	survive	X	X
	waste		

Matching

Match each word in the left column with its opposite meanings in the right column.

____	1. survive	a. disappoint
____	2. self-reliant	b. boring
____	3. foolish	c. use
____	4. shelter	d. die
____	5. admire	e. wise
____	6. waste	f. think badly of
____	7. adventurous	g. needy
____	8. impress	h. unprotect

Word Forms

Read the sentences. Change the incorrect word form in bold to the correct form.

________________ 1. Alaska is a place of **impression** beauty. Not many places are as beautiful as Alaska.

________________ 2. One example of **self-reliant** is growing your own food. This means you don't need to buy vegetables at the market.

________________ 3. Do you **admirable** McCandless for giving away a large amount of money to help others?

________________ 4. My parents enjoyed their **adventurous** in Africa.

________________ 5. In Africa, they stayed dry when in rained because they had a tent for a **sheltered.**

________________ 6. I think people who do not recycle **wasteful** resources.

________________ 7. If you are a **foolish,** you never make plans for the future.

________________ 8. People need water in the desert for their **survive.**

Vocabulary Use

Vocabulary Note

Some of the target vocabulary in Chapter 5 has usages and meanings that are different from how they were used in the reading. To become a better reader, make sure you understand these phrase/usages:

admire *admirable qualities*

shelter *to lead a sheltered existence* (kept away from bad things)

True or False

Write T if the statement is true and F if the statement is false.

____ 1. Some people don't like to have adventures because they are afraid.

____ 2. Children learn to be self-reliant when their parents help them.

____ 3. It is impossible to survive a natural disaster such as an earthquake or flood.

____ 4. Many people will be impressed if you are able to climb a very high mountain.

____ 5. The more mistakes you make, the more admirable you are.

____ 6. If you waste time, you are able to finish many things.

____ 7. In most cultures, people have found a way to meet their need for shelter.

____ 8. A person can avoid being foolish by asking others for advice.

Write about It

Write a paragraph in response to this prompt. Try to use at least three of the words from the chart on page 59.

Henry David Thoreau once wrote, "Go confidently in the direction of your dreams! Live the life you've imagined." What kind of life do you dream about having? Do you imagine a simple life that is close to nature, or a busy life with many exciting activities? Describe the life of your dreams.

CHAPTER

6

Saving Antarctica

Getting Ready to Read

Antarctica is the continent at the most southern point on Earth. It is usually the coldest place on the planet. It is surrounded by the Southern Ocean. With a classmate, check the items that you think relate in some way to Antarctica. Be prepared to explain your answers.

____ humidity	____ polar bears
____ icebergs	____ scientists
____ native people	____ tourists
____ ozone hole	____ towns
____ penguins	____ whales

Vocabulary Preview

For each sentence, choose one of the words or phrases to match the meaning of the word in bold.

ate	pulled out
completed	take possession of
illegal	tolerate
lead	using, often in a bad way

1. I **accomplished** a lot today. I cleaned the bathroom, went shopping, did my homework, and wrote a letter to my parents.

   I think **accomplished** means ____________________________________.

2. No country can **claim** Antarctica as its own, but several countries have said that certain parts of the continent belong to them.

   I think **claim** means ____.

3. My boss asked me to **conduct** the meeting this afternoon. I don't like it, but I can't say no to my boss.

   I think **conduct** means ______________________________________.

4. Henry was so hungry after skiing that he **consumed** nearly all the food in the refrigerator.

   I think **consumed** means _____________________________________.

5. I moved from Hawaii to New England, where the winters are very cold. I had to **endure** the snow storms until I bought a warm coat.

   I think **endure** means _______________________________________.

6. The forests of Northern California have trees that are over more than 1,000 years old, but logging companies in the past cut them down to sell. However, this **exploitation** of the forests was stopped before all the trees were gone.

   I think **exploitation** means ___________________________________.

7. I went to the dentist because I had a toothache. She said that the tooth was bad. After she **extracted** it, the pain was gone.

   I think **extracted** means ______________________________________.

8. Smoking is **prohibited** in most public places in California. You can't smoke in restaurants, theaters, sporting arenas, or stores.

   I think **prohibited** means ______________________________________.

Reading Skill

Skill **Parts of a Dictionary Entry**

Purpose To be able to use all the information in a dictionary entry

Example & Explanation

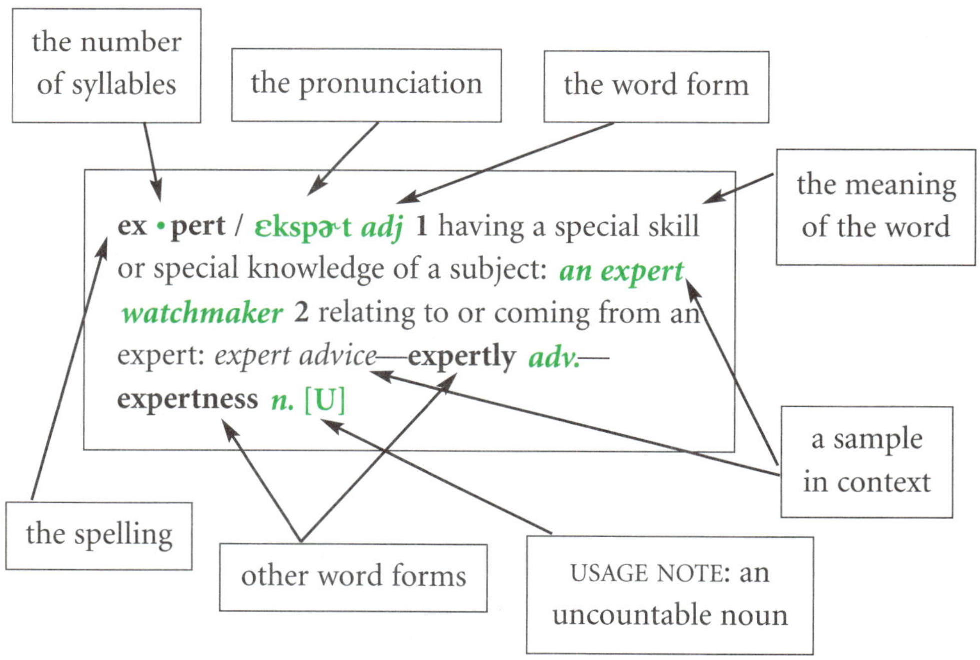

Identifying Parts of a Dictionary Entry

Draw an arrow from each question box to the place in the entry where you can find the answer.

1.

the type of word	usage information

> **com • merce** /'kɑmɚs / *n.* [U] **1** the buying and selling of goods and services: *interstate commerce* (= among U.S. states) **2** OLD-FASHIONED relationships and communication between people

the meaning of the word	a sample in context

2.

the pronunciation	the number of syllables

> **mo • tive** /moʊtɪv/ n. [C] something or someone that makes you want to do or achieve something, especially when the reason is kept hidden: *Police say the motive for the killing was an unpaid drug debt.*—**motiveless** *adj.*

the spelling	other word forms

Skimming Practice

Skim the reading on pages 67–68 to find the main idea of each paragraph. Write the paragraph number next to the correct answer.

____ Humans have known about Antarctica since 1773.

____ Shirley Metz and others have worked to keep the continent safe from exploitation.

____ Shirley Metz skied across Antarctica to get a good reputation as someone who knows the continent.

Reading

Shirley Metz: The First Woman to Ski to the South Pole

(1) On January 17, 1989, Shirley Metz and six other skiers (one other woman and five men) reached the South Pole in Antarctica. It was the first time that a woman or any American had skied to the South Pole. The trip covered 750 miles and took two and a half months. The group **endured** temperatures of 38 degrees below zero and winds of up to 140 miles. They skied eight to nine hours a day. Each skier had to **consume** 7,000 calories a day to keep warm and to have enough energy to ski. Metz, who is a thin woman, couldn't eat as much as the others, so she ate sticks of butter. For Metz and the others, it was a difficult journey. However, Metz's goal was more than just **accomplishing** the journey. She wanted to be known as an expert on Antarctica. This would allow her to speak out about saving the unspoiled continent from **exploitation.**

(2) The first human being to see Antarctica was James Cook, who sailed around it in 1773. He was unimpressed and stated that it was useless. In the 1800s and early 1900s, many explorers sailed to the continent. Their goals were to reach the continent and survive. They were not concerned with saving it for later generations. In fact, many who reached Antarctica saw great commercial possibilities there. Whaling ships, which were designed to capture whales and process them, followed and hunted whales and seals almost to extinction.* In the mid-1900s, scientists began to realize the importance of Antarctica, and in 1959, a treaty** was signed to protect it. The treaty states

---

***extinction**—*n.* when an animal or something stops existing

****treaty**—*n.* an agreement between countries

that all countries are free to **conduct** scientific research as long as it does no harm to the continent, its animals, or its resources. To date, 43 nations have signed the treaty.

(3) Metz, however, knew that there were countries and companies that had more than a scientific interest in Antarctica. Owners of some ships **claimed** to take whales and other animals for scientific research, but their true motives were commercial. Some signers of the treaty wanted to **extract** oil and minerals. She knew that if she had personal experience in Antarctica, she could give lectures and write articles. She hoped that the world community would listen to her and stand behind her in protecting this beautiful place. So far, because of Shirley Metz's efforts and the efforts countless other scientists and everyday people, Antarctica remains pristine.*** The treaty now **prohibits** any commercial use of the continent until 2048.

***pristine—*adj.* unspoiled, pure

Reading Comprehension

Circle the letter of the correct answer or write a short answer.

1. How many people were in Shirley Metz's group?
   a. 5
   b. 6
   c. 7

2. Which of these statements is true?
   a. The skiers had to eat sticks of butter in order to stay warm.
   b. The skiers skied at a rate of 300 miles per month.
   c. Every day the temperature was 38 degrees.

3. James Cook believed that there was nothing of value in Antarctica.
   a. true
   b. false
   c. The reading doesn't say.
4. In the 1800s, explorers who were interested in developing Antarctica for commercial use were the only ones who took the risk of such a dangerous journey.
   a. true
   b. false
   c. The reading doesn't say.
5. What types of animals live in Antarctica? ______________________________
6. When did scientists start to be concerned about the future of Antarctica?
   a. Between 1900 and 1940
   b. Between 1940 and 1960
   c. After 1960
7. For how many total years does the treaty protect Antarctica? ________________
8. How many countries have signed the treaty? ____________________________
9. What does Shirley Metz do to help protect Antarctica? ____________________

   ____
10. Since her trip in 1979, Metz has returned to Antarctica many times.
    a. true
    b. false
    c. The reading doesn't say.

Discuss Your Ideas

In small groups, discuss the answers to these questions. Be prepared to share your answers with the class.

1. Do you think that Shirley Metz made a difference in how people think about Antarctica? Do you agree with the idea that one person can make a difference in the world?
2. What commercial use does Antarctica have? Do you think that countries should be allowed to develop Antarctica? What kind of development should be allowed?
3. What other natural places are being exploited today? How are some people trying to stop this?

STUDY TIP

Managing Your Study Time

Studying all night before a test can often work well. However, once the test is over, the information is usually quickly forgotten. Studying on a regular basis for relatively short periods of time (1 to 2 hours) is much better for remembering information.

Vocabulary Comprehension

With a classmate, fill in the empty boxes in the chart. Do not write anything in the boxes that have an X. You can use an English dictionary.

Nouns	Verbs	Adjectives	Adverbs
	accomplish		X
claim		X	X
	conduct	X	X
	consume		X
	endure	1. 2.	X
exploitation		1. 2.	X
extract	X	X	
prohibit			

Sentence Completion

Fill in each blank with one of the words from the chart on page 71. Use the context to help you choose the correct form of the word.

Antarctic Penguins

Since 1959, the Antarctic Treaty has protected the 17 species of penguins that live in Antarctica. The treaty ① ____________________ any kind of oil or mineral drilling. However, it allows scientists to ② ____________________ research as long as they do not harm animals or ③ ____________________ them for other uses. In addition, the scientists cannot ④ ____________________ any animal from its habitat and place it somewhere else.

Emperor penguins are one of the most recognizable species of penguins in Antarctica. Once two penguins ⑤ ____________________ each other as mates, they are together for life. They are driven to ⑥ ____________________ their goal of making a baby penguin every year. Once the females lay their eggs, the males keep the eggs warm throughout the winter. The males must ⑦ ____________________ months of cold and darkness. Meanwhile, the female tries to ⑧ ____________________ as much food as she can find in the ocean. When the spring comes, the female finds her mate and takes over caring for the egg. The males can then make their way to the ocean to feed.

Odd One Out

Circle the word that does not belong in each group. Be prepared to explain why the word does not belong.

1. consume, build, use, eat
2. examine, exploit, quiz, test
3. conduct, goal, lead, manage
4. complaint, endurance, patience, strength
5. allow, let, permit, prohibit
6. accomplishment, achievement, frustration, success
7. extract, insert, add, include
8. claim, declare, deny, insist

Vocabulary Use

Vocabulary Note

Some of the target vocabulary in Chapter 6 has usages and meanings that are different from how they were used in the reading. To become a better reader, make sure you understand these phrase/usages:

accomplish *an accomplished pianist* (highly skilled)

claim *a claim to fame, to make a claim* (demand as having a right to)

conduct *to conduct,* but *someone's conduct* (behavior)

exploits *someone's exploits* (unusual or brave acts)

Short Answer

Write an answer to these questions. Try to use the word in bold in your answer.

1. What is a significant **accomplishment** that has affected modern society?

   ____

2. What types of products can **consumers** find in a supermarket?

   ____

3. What does the law **prohibit** drivers from doing?

   ____

4. What kind of weather do people in Alaska **endure** in winter?

   ____

Write about It

Write a paragraph in response to this prompt. Try to use at least three of the words from the chart on page 71 in this assignment.

Roald Amundsen (1872–1928) was the first person to reach both the North and South poles. He wrote that success comes to the one "who has everything in order—luck, people call it." Do you agree with Amundsen's idea of success? Why or why not?

Vocabulary Skill	
Skill	**Four Techniques for Understanding the Meanings of Words in Context**
Purpose	To spend less time looking words up in a dictionary and more time reading
Explanation	One of the best ways to become a better reader in English is to learn how to guess the meanings of words by looking at the context of the word. Sometimes, this will give you enough that the word makes sense. There are four techniques that can be helpful.

Technique 1	**Look at the punctuation.**
	Sometimes a synonym or definition of word comes after the word surrounded by commas or parentheses. Capital letters usually indicate the name of someone or something.
Examples	**I am *training,* or teaching, my dog how to sit up.**
	Tourists can go downtown on the *shuttle* (a small bus).
Technique 2	**Look for the word *which* or *that.***
	This word is often followed by clauses that may explain more about the word.
Example	**Shirley walked on *El Camino,* which is the ancient trail in Northern Spain.**
Technique 3	**Use your knowledge of the world.**
	Instead of going to a dictionary, look around the word and try to figure out the context. Ask yourself what idea makes sense given everything else in the sentence.
Examples	**You can look at the *schedules* online, so you won't have to wait at the bus stop very long.**
	I can't *hang out* at the cafe. I have to go to the travel agent.
Technique 4	**Tolerate vagueness.**
	This is the most important technique, but it is also the hardest. When you read, you want to understand everything, but, in truth, you do not need to know the exact meaning of every word to understand a reading passage.
Example	Read this passage. There are words you may not know, but if you can say what the main idea is, that's enough for a first reading. You shouldn't have to look up any words.
	If you want to become a power walker, you should know the dos and don'ts. Do stand erect. Don't look down. Do swing your arms front and back. Don't move your arms back and forth. Do push off from your toes and land on your heel. Don't take long strides. Do walk fast. Don't get out of breath.

Learning Meanings from Context

Read the passage.

Traveling West

In the mid-nineteenth century, many easterners decided to find their **fortune** by heading west, which was almost the ends of the earth for them. In truth, very few found riches, and some **succumbed** (died) to the **grueling** journey. But some did find a **plot** to live on. The best part was that they didn't have to pay for the land. In 1862, the Congress passed the Homestead Act, which gave land in the west to individuals who would **cultivate** it. If the settlers grew a crop, they could become the owners of the property after a few years. To get to the west, many people traveled by covered wagon train. Unlike what has been **depicted** in movies and on television, the wagon train experience was very difficult. Indeed, most travelers found themselves walking most of the time because the wagon wasn't **sturdy** enough to carry them and their belongings as well.

Write a synonym or short definition of each word in bold. Use the techniques described in the box on pages 74–75 to help you. Do not use a dictionary.

1. fortune ______________________________
2. succumbed ______________________________
3. grueling ______________________________
4. plot ______________________________
5. cultivate ______________________________
6. depicted ______________________________
7. sturdy ______________________________

Timed Reading

Read the passage according to your teacher's instructions. Then answer the questions on page 211 without looking at the reading.

Alaska and Hawaii

Both Alaska and Hawaii had native populations when Europeans arrived. The natives of both places lost their independence to the United States. Both Alaska and Hawaii became states in 1959. And, Alaska and Hawaii are the only states separated from the rest of the U.S. They are both popular tourist destinations. However, despite these similarities, Alaska and Hawaii are very different from each other.

The United States purchased Alaska from Russia in 1884. At that time, a lot of people thought that buying Alaska wasn't a good idea. Then, gold was
* discovered there in 1890, and people went there as fast as they could. Some stayed, but most didn't. Today, even though Alaska is the largest state, it has less than a million people. The people of Alaska are mostly white, but about 15 percent are natives. Alaskans are fond of the outdoors and love the vast Alaskan wilderness. The weather in Alaska is very cold in the winter. It is also dark for up to sixteen hours a day because it is so far north. Therefore, people spend time outdoors in the spring and summer months. The temperatures
* are cool, but there can be 20 hours of daylight. Popular outdoor activities include hiking, climbing, skiing, hunting, and fishing.

In contrast to Alaska, Hawaii became part of the United States because of trade. Hawaii's climate was perfect for growing sugar, and the U.S. wanted sugar. As a result, in 1874, Hawaii and the U.S. signed a trading agreement. Hawaii doesn't have a lot of land like Alaska, but its string of islands is 1,500 miles long. There are about 1.3 million people living in Hawaii, so there are

more Hawaiians than Alaskans. But, while Alaska has about one person per square mile, Hawaii has almost 200! In addition, the population in Hawaii is
* more varied than the population in Alaska. About one-third of Hawaiians are Asian American, and one-third are European American. However, native Hawaiians are only 9 percent of the population. Hawaii is a popular place to visit since it is closer to the equator and the weather changes less. Therefore, Hawaii offers year-round outdoor activities that revolve around the ocean and its gorgeous beaches. They include deep sea fishing, scuba diving, wind surfing, and sunbathing.

In short, Alaska and Hawaii are certainly different from the other 48 states but their biggest differences are from each other.

UNIT 4

Unusual Jobs

Jobs, such as teacher, lawyer, nurse, truck driver and accountant, are common. Probably you know someone who has one of these jobs. But some jobs are not common. In fact, some jobs are so unusual that you have never heard of them.

With a classmate, match the job on the left with its description on the right.

____ 1. forest fire lookout	a. watches birds so that they don't kill each other
____ 2. furniture tester	b. watches for trees on fire
____ 3. gum buster	c. takes the poison out of a deadly animal
____ 4. life coach	d. sits in and out of sofas and chairs
____ 5. ostrich babysitter	e. removes sticky substances from under chairs
____ 6. pet detective	f. puts an advertisement in the air
____ 7. sky writer	g. helps people make decisions
____ 8. snake milker	h. finds animals that are lost

Do any of these jobs seem interesting to you? What other unusual jobs can you think of?

CHAPTER

7

Life Coaches

Getting Reading to Read

Discuss these questions with a partner.

1. Who do you ask for advice from when you have a problem?
2. Who usually asks you for advice?
3. What qualifications does a person need to be able to give advice?
4. What advice do you have for: a classmate who is having trouble with a class; a friend who needs to earn money for school; a family member who can't sleep much at night.

Vocabulary Preview

For each sentence, choose one of the words or phrases to match the meaning of the word in bold.

belief in oneself	money owed
come out of	pressure
focus on	pushed or encouraged
give a job to	suggestions

1. When I don't know what to do, I always ask my father for **advice**. He is a wise man, and he always leads me in the right direction.

   I think **advice** means ______________________________.

2. Sometimes the difference between an average athlete and a great one is **confidence**. It is more important than ability.

   I think **confidence** means ______________________________.

3. People sometimes lose their houses because of their **debt**.

   I think **debt** means ______________________________.

4. The audience members could not wait for the rock star to **emerge** from the big box on stage.

   I think **emerge** means ______________________________.

5. Great news! The company wants to **hire** me!

   I think **hire** means ______________________________.

6. The movie about electric cars **motivated** me to buy one.

   I think **motivated** means ______________________________.

7. Oncologists are doctors that **specialize** in cancer. They are experts.

   I think **specialize** means ____.

8. When you have a lot of **stress,** one thing you can do is sit down, close your eyes, and take several deep breaths.

   I think **stress** means ____.

Reading Skill

Skill	**Asking Questions as You Read**
Purpose	To understand a reading better by being an active reader
Explanation	Good readers think when they read. They ask questions as they read and look for answers. They don't stop at each word. Instead, they read the whole text several times and think about what they are reading.
Example	In recent years, a new kind of coaching job has emerged, but it doesn't have anything to do with sports. It's a life coach. **Questions** What is a life coach? How is it different from a sports coach?

Asking Questions

Read these sentences. Think about them, and then write a question. Then read the text on pages 83 and 84.

1. There are many reasons to hire a life coach.

   ____

2. Perhaps you spend more money than you have, so you have a lot of debt.

   ____

Reading

Life Coaches

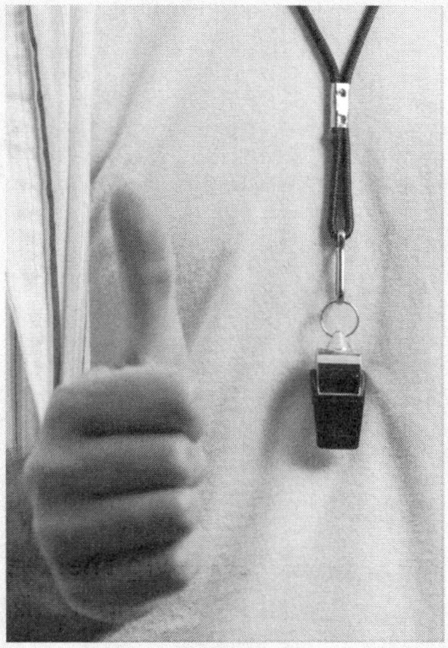

Having a good coach is very important to a sports team. Anyone who watches or plays a sport knows this. The coach of a team is a director, a **motivator**, and a trainer. A good coach can help lead a team to victory, but a bad coach can help cause a team to fail.

In recent years, a new kind of coaching job has **emerged**, but it doesn't have anything to do with sports. It's a life coach. Like sports coaches, life coaches direct, **motivate,** and train their clients.* Unlike sport coaches, life coaches do not make decisions for clients or tell clients what to do. Their support is limited to **advice** and encouragement in order help their clients achieve a goal that they have set for themselves.

Why would someone want to hire a life coach? There are as many reasons as there are goals that a person has. For example, if you are unhappy with your job, but you don't know how to find a job that is just right for you, you can **hire** a life coach that **specializes** in helping people find satisfying jobs. Perhaps you spend more money than you have, so you have a lot of **debt**. You know you have to stop spending money and make a budget,** but you don't know how. A life coach that **specializes** in financial matters can help you. Maybe you have lost a loved one, and you can't stop feeling sad. Bereavement*** coaches can help you feel better. Other life coaches help with losing weight, getting a divorce, advancing your career, reducing **stress**, building **confidence**, and even finding the right person to marry.

---

*__client__—*n.* a person who gets help from an expert or professional

**__budget__—*n.* a financial plan

***__bereavement__—*n.* the sadness you feel when someone dies

In short, life coaches can help you achieve any goal that you may have. You just have to be willing to accept someone's help. And, if that is a problem for you, there is a life coach who **specializes** in helping people accept help from others!

Reading Comprehension

Circle the letter of the correct answer, or write a short answer.

1. A sports coach can make the difference between winning a game and losing a game.
   a. true
   b. false
   c. unknown
2. A life coach and a sports coach are alike because
   a. they both motivate people.
   b. they both cost a lot of money.
   c. they both are successful.
3. A life coach is unlike a sports coach because
   a. a life coach can sometimes fail.
   b. a life coach doesn't make decisions.
   c. a life coach must be a woman.
4. A client goes to a life coach to figure out what his or her problem is.
   a. true
   b. false
   c. The reading doesn't say.
5. Life coaches usually specialize in many areas.
   a. true
   b. false
   c. The reading doesn't say.

6. More women than men go to life coaches for help.
   a. true
   b. false
   c. The reading doesn't say.
7. How many types of life coaches does the article mention?
   a. 2–3
   b. 6–9
   c. 10–11
8. You can guess from the article that there is a life coach for almost every problem that a person might have.
   a. true
   b. false
   c. unknown

Discuss Your Ideas

In small groups, discuss the answers to these questions. Be prepared to share your answers with the class.

1. Match the problem in the left column with an appropriate life coach in the right column. More than one answer could be possible.

I'm lonely.	job/career
My dog died.	meeting people/dating
I weigh 300 pounds.	health issues
My spouse left me.	bereavement
I want a raise.	divorce
I hate my boss.	interpersonal skills

2. What kind of advice do you think each specialist gives?
3. What other kinds of problems could a life coach help people with?
4. Would you like to go to a life coach? Why or why not?

STUDY TIP

Checking Your Spelling

Checking your spelling is easy when you write on a computer. If you see a red line under a word, it means that the word is misspelled. Put the cursor on the word and right click. You will see a list of suggestions. Left click on the correct spelling, and the computer will insert the correctly spelled word.

Vocabulary Comprehension

With a classmate, fill in the empty boxes in the chart. Do not write anything in the boxes that have an X. You can use an English dictionary.

Nouns	Verbs	Adjectives	Adverbs
1. advice 2.			X
confidence	X		
1. debt 2.	X	X	X
	emerge		X
X	hire	X	X
1. 2.	motivate		X
1. 2.	specialize		X
stress			

Matching

Match each word in the left column with its opposite in the right column.

____ 1. advise		a. fire
____ 2. confidence		b. uncertainty
____ 3. debt		c. disappear
____ 4. emerge		d. relaxation
____ 5. hire		e. discourage
____ 6. motivate		f. suggest
____ 7. stress		g. money paid

Word Forms

Fill in each blank with the correct form of the words. Use the context to help you. One word in each set will not be used.

1. **advice, advisor, advisable**

   Did your ____________________ give you good ____________________?

2. **confidence, confident, confidently**

   Speakers should walk ____________________ to the front of the room and begin talking. I want to be that ____________________ in front of an audience.

3. **motivation, motivate**

   A computer company wants to ____________________ its workers by offering a $500 prize for the best name for a new product.

4. **specialization, specialist, specializes**

   I need a lawyer that ____________________ in tax problems. I am glad that my friend's brother is a tax ____________________.

5. **stress, stressful, stressfully**

   Tests can be very ____________________, even if I have studied hard.

Vocabulary Use

Vocabulary Note

Some of the target vocabulary in Chapter 7 has usages and meanings that are different from how they were used in the reading. To become a better reader, make sure you understand these phrase/usages:

debt *to be in debt, to be in someone's debt*

True or False

Write T if the statement is true and F if the statement is false.

____ 1. If you aren't confident about speaking a new language, you avoid using it on the phone.

____ 2. Motivation is why people don't do anything.

____ 3. When you are stressed, you need to rest.

____ 4. People in debt have a lot of money.

____ 5. Many people get advice from their best friends.

____ 6. When a bird emerges from its shell, it is very hungry.

Write about It

Read the statement. Write a paragraph in response to this prompt. Try to use three words from the chart on page 86.

Some home-based jobs include working as a customer service agent, online tutor, or website designer. Are you interested in a home-based job? What are the advantages and disadvantages?

CHAPTER

8

Skywriters

Getting Ready to Read

There are many types of advertisements. An advertisement gives people information about a product or service. Discuss these questions in small groups.

1. What kinds of advertisements do you see most often?

    ____ billboard

    ____ television

    ____ Internet

    ____ newspaper

    ____ magazine

    ____ sky-writing (white letters in the sky)

2. Which type of advertising do you think works the best? Why?

Vocabulary Preview

For each sentence, choose one of the words or phrases to match the meaning of the word in bold.

career requiring a specific education	people who create messages to sell products
encouraging strongly	said publicly
look at something for a long time	typical
not used much anymore	very interesting

1. Every year, Mike's state hold a meeting for his **profession.**

   I think **profession** means ______________________________.

2. Billboards are **common** on the sides of roads or highways.

   I think **common** means ______________________________.

3. **Advertisers** are always looking to new ways to get people's attention.

   I think **advertisers** means ______________________________.

4. Computer keyboards were developed from typewriters, which are now **old-fashioned.**

   I think **old-fashioned** means ______________________________.

5. The president **declared** today a national holiday.

   I think **declared** means ______________________________.

6. Some people like to sit on the beach and **stare** at the ocean.

   I think **stare** means ______________________________.

7. My friends are **urging** me to visit Hawaii, but I don't like to travel by plane.

   I think **urging** means ______________________________.

8. Have you ever found the different shapes of clouds in the sky **intriguing**?

   I think **intriguing** means ______________________________.

Reading Skill

Skill	**Thinking as You Read: Making Connections to Experience**
Purpose	To understand a reading better by connecting it to your own experience
Explanation	Good readers think about what they read. They make connections to their own experiences. In other words, they think about how information in the reading is related to things they have seen and done in their own lives.
Example	Skywriting pilots make white letters in the sky. Sometimes these letters spell messages urging people to buy a certain brand of car or type of soft drink. **Making Connection Questions** 1. **Have I ever seen skywriting? What kind of messages have I seen? Can I imagine what skywriting looks like?** 2. **How often do I see messages urging someone to buy cars or soft drinks?**

Making Connections

Read these sentences from the reading. Then write a connection to your own experience.

1. People spend plenty of time looking at skywriting messages because they can be readable for up to ten minutes. This is very good for advertisers, who want people to spend as much attention as possible.

   ____

   ____

2. In a world full of messages, the words up high in the blue sky are very intriguing, and the skill that it takes to make them is very impressive.

   ____

   ____

Skimming Practice

Skim the reading to find the main idea of each paragraph. Write the paragraph number next to the correct answer.

_____ Skywriting is an intriguing way to write messages in today's world.

_____ Andy Stinis' family is still in the skywriting business.

_____ The story of skywriters is interesting.

_____ As an advertiser, Pepsi Cola liked Andy Stinis's skywriting because people paid attention to it.

_____ Suzanne Asbery-Oliver is another skywriter who writes bigger letters in the sky.

Reading

The Story of Skywriters

(1) Have you ever seen white letters in the sky that spell a message? In the United States, these messages are **common** in the sky above large public beaches or sporting events. They are sometimes messages **urging** people to buy a certain brand of car or a type of soft drink or to visit a certain business. At times, they are romantic messages that **declare** love or ask for marriage. Who writes these messages in the sky? The story of skywriters is an interesting one.

(2) In 1931, pilot Andy Stinis wrote messages for Pepsi-Cola. This company realized that skywriting was a good form of communication because it got people's attention. To understand skywriting, people have to **stare** at the sky and watch to see which letters will appear. This means that people pay more attention than they **normally** do to other kinds of **advertisements**. People spend time looking at skywriting messages because they can be readable for up to ten minutes. This is very good for **advertisers**, who want people to pay as much attention as possible.

(3) Today, Andy Stinis' son and grandson are skywriters by **profession.** Their company, Skytypers, is a company that prints messages in the sky. These messages are clear and easy to read because they look like the printing of a type of printer that creates letters by moving back and forth like an **old-fashioned** typewriter.

(4) Another interesting example of a skywriter is Suzanne Asbery-Oliver, a female pilot who writes messages in the sky that can be as long as 10 miles across. She flies up to 14,000 miles to create messages that people can see for more than 30 miles from any direction on the ground. To create each word, she spends at least ten minutes of careful flying and turning.

(5) If you ever see a skywriting message in the sky, think about this: Who is the pilot making sure that the message is clear? Would you like to be a skywriter? In a world full of messages, the words in the blue sky are **intriguing** to people, and the skill that it takes to create them is very impressive.

Reading Comprehension

Circle the letter of the correct answer, or write a short answer.

1. Skywriting is seen in the United States at
   a. sports events
   b. beaches
   c. both a and b
2. Skywriting is used in advertisements. In what other ways is skywriting used?

   ____
3. Which company used skywriting back in 1931? ____________________
4. The main advantage of skywriting as a form of advertising is that it makes people
   a. notice the product
   b. stare at the sky
   c. guess letters as they appear
5. How long can skywriting messages last? ____________________
6. What can we guess about the Stinis family members?
   a. They were very close to each other.
   b. They made a lot of money in skywriting.
   c. The younger members followed Andy Stinis' example.

7. What reason can you give for your answer to Question 6?

____

8. The skills of a skywriting pilot include being able to
   a. create large messages
   b. fly high
   c. both a and b

Discuss Your Ideas

In small groups, discuss the answers to these questions. Be prepared to share your answers with the class.

1. Do you enjoy riding in airplanes? Why or why not?
2. Have you ever thought about being a pilot?
3. Can you think of any other unusual jobs that are related to flying or being a pilot?
4. Imagine that you have the chance to create a personal skywriting message. What kind of message would you create? Where would you like the message to appear?

STUDY TIP

Taking Notes While You Read

Taking notes while you read will help you remember important information more easily. Here are some tips on how to take notes.

1. Read with a pen and paper. (You can also take notes on a computer.)
2. Underline or highlight important information or mark it with a star.
3. Write notes about the most important information (names, numbers, dates, definitions, etc.). Use abbreviations to save time; for example, you can use an arrow pointing upward (↑) to represent the word *increase*.

Make sure that your notes are clear and organized in a way that will help you to understand them later.

Vocabulary Comprehension

With a classmate, fill in the empty boxes in the chart. Do not write anything in the boxes that have an X. You can use an English dictionary.

Nouns	Verbs	Adjectives	Adverbs
1. advertiser 2.			X
X	X		commonly
	declare	X	X
		1. intriguing 2.	X
X	X	old-fashioned	X
1. professional 2. 3.	X		
	stare	X	X
1. 2.	urge		

Sentence Completion

Fill in each blank with one of the words from the chart on page 96. Use the context to help you choose the correct form of the word.

1. Why do ________________ like to hire skywriters?
2. Television commercials are probably the most ________________ advertisement in the U.S.
3. People sometimes give flowers as a ________________ of their feelings.
4. Skywriting messages ________________ me whenever they appear in the sky. Who are they for?
5. If you wear strange clothing, other people may ________________.
6. Some advertisements ________________ people to buy a product to make their lives better.
7. It's important to be creative in the advertising ________________.
8. You can find advertisements that are ________________ in newspapers from the 1900s.

Odd One Out

Circle the word or phrase that does not belong in each group. Be prepared to explain why the word does not belong.

1. profession, recreation, vocation, occupation
2. outdated, old-fashioned, up-to-date, old
3. stare, glance, watch, gaze
4. deny, express, state, declare
5. common, normal, former, typical
6. fascinate, interest, intrigue, bore
7. advertise, hide, cover, keep quiet
8. urgent, unimportant, necessary, immediate

Vocabulary Use

Vocabulary Note

Some of the target vocabulary in Chapter 8 has usages and meanings that are different from how they were used in the reading. To become a better reader, make sure you understand these phrase/usages:

declare *to declare goods at customs*

intrigue *a web of intrigue* (secret plans)

urge *a sense of urgency/to be urgent* (needing immediate attention)

Short Answer

Write an answer to these questions. Try to use the word in bold in your answer.

1. What might happen if you **stare** at the sun too long? ______________________
2. Why do mothers **urge** their children to eat nutritious food such as vegetables?
 ____
3. How do you know if someone is **intrigued** by a book? ______________________
 ____
4. What kind of flowers are used to **declare** love in the United States? ___________
5. Why are **advertisers** interested in communicating with as many people as possible? ____

Write about It

Write a paragraph in response to the prompt. Try to use at least three of the words from the chart on page 96 in this assignment.

Look at the unusual jobs listed on page 79. Imagine that you are an employer. You are going to interview someone for one of these jobs. Write a list of five interview questions. For example, an employer may ask what someone enjoys about the profession of snake milking.

Vocabulary Skill

Skill	**Learning Suffixes**
Purpose	To help with understanding words
Explanation	Suffixes are parts of words that can be added to the end of a base or root word to change the type of word—or part of speech—it is.
Examples	Noun suffixes: ***-ance, -ence, -er, -ity, -ment , -ness, -tion, -sion***
	Verb suffixes: ***-ate, -en, -ify, -fy, -ize,***
	Adjective suffixes: ***-able, -ible, -al, -ive, -ful, -less, -ous***

Identifying Word Types

Determine the word type for each word by looking at the suffix. Write N for noun, V for verb, and ADJ for adjective.

____ 1. baker

____ 2. concession

____ 3. edible

____ 4. eradicate

____ 5. fanciful

6. ____ harmonize

7. ____ maintenance

8. ____ nutritious

9. ____ terrify

10. ____ veracity

Recognizing Suffixes

Work with a classmate to fill in this chart. Don't use a dictionary. If you can't think of a word with the suffix, skip it.

Suffix	Word Type	Example	Your Example
-able, -ible	*adjective*	recyclable	*enjoyable*
-al		professional	
-ance, -ence		resistance	
-ate		appreciate	
-en		darken	
-er		teacher	
-fy, -ify		verify	
-ful		restful	
-ity		obesity	
-ive		positive	
-ize		memorize	
-less		effortless	
-ment		equipment	
-ness		kindness	
-ous		generous	
-tion, -sion		transportation	

Timed Reading

Read the passage according to your teacher's instructions. Then answer the questions on page 212 without looking at the reading.

Training Wild Animals

A lot of children often dream of working with animals when they grow up. As adults, a few actually do find careers in the animal world. They quickly discover that working with animals can be fun and rewarding, but it takes a lot of education and hard work. There are many jobs in the animal world, such as veterinarians, groomers, and zoo keepers. One of the most popular, however, is a wild animal trainer.

Becoming a wild animal trainer starts with love for and commitment to wild animals. Trainers also need to learn about the behavior of the type of * animal they want to work with. They take classes in biology, zoology, and animal psychology. The trainers have to be aware their animal is dangerous. Even if the relationship between a trainer and an animal seems good, these animals are wild and can attack at any time. Also, finding a job as a wild animal trainer is hard, so would-be trainers should volunteer at zoos and wild-animal sanctuaries. Volunteering provides hands-on experience in the care and well-being of the animal. Plus, paying jobs often go to experienced volunteers.

Trainers also need several personal characteristics. The most important is * having compassion for the animals, but it is also very important to be in top physical shape. Animal trainers are very active, and anyone who wants to be an animal trainer has to love the outdoors and be very strong. Since most jobs in animal training require interaction with the public, an animal trainer must also be able to relate well to strangers and to communicate clearly and knowledgeably. The most visible animal trainer jobs are at zoos and amusement parks. Parks such as Sea World have several sea mammal trainers that work with dolphins and whales.

* Circuses have trainers for lions, bears, and elephants. Wild animal trainers can also find work in television shows and in movies. In all these places, the animals do amazing tricks. The connection between the animal and trainer seems real and caring. However, to get to that point, a trainer may have to work hours each day for over a year with their animal. The training takes a lot of repetition and rewards.

In short, the life of a wild animal trainer takes knowledge, hard work, and time. But, for the child who had a dream, it is the best job in the world.

UNIT 5

Towns with a Purpose

Towns and cities around the world are famous for different reasons. For example, Hollywood is famous for movies and movies stars, and London is famous because the Queen of England lives there.

With a classmate, discuss why these cities are well-known. Then add two cities that you know and discuss why they are famous. Be prepared to tell the class about the cities you added.

1. Bangkok
2. Beijing
3. Cairo
4. Dubai
5. Mexico City
6. Rio de Janeiro
7. San Francisco
8. Tokyo
9. ______________________
10. ______________________

CHAPTER

9

Gilroy, California

Getting Ready to Read

With a classmate, discuss these four proverbs about garlic. What do you think each means?

1. Garlic is as good as ten mothers.
2. You cannot trust anyone who does not eat garlic.
3. Garlic is not only a flavor; it is the secret of happiness.
4. There is no such thing as a little garlic.

Do you have a proverb about garlic or another food in your native language? Be prepared to share your proverbs with the class.

Vocabulary Preview

For each sentence, choose one of the words or phrases to match the meaning of the word in bold.

awaited	showing
helps	something specific
love and care	turn in
not making money	was in charge of

1. Every year, one of the most highly **anticipated** events on campus is the first home football game. The students are excited!

   I think **anticipated** means ____________________________________.

2. Exercising regularly **benefits** your heart. It becomes stronger and will last longer.

   I think **benefits** means ____________________________________.

3. In my photography class today, the teacher was **demonstrating** the best way to make photos bigger. I learned a lot.

   I think **demonstrating** means ____________________________________.

4. My brother's **devotion** to our father was amazing. He did everything for him when he was sick.

   I think **devotion** means ____________________________________.

5. For my retirement, my boss **hosted** a party and invited the whole staff.

   I think **hosted** means ____________________________________.

6. After the 2011 earthquake in Japan, people from all over the world sent money to **non-profit** organizations like the Red Cross.

   I think **non-profit** means ____________________________________.

7. I collect toy pigs. I like to find new ones at **specialty** shops.

   I think **specialty** means ____________________________________.

8. "You must **submit** your paper by Tuesday," said the teacher. "If you don't turn in your paper by then, I will not accept it."

   I think **submit** means ____________________________________.

Reading Skill

Skill	**Making Predictions as You Read**
Purpose	To understand a reading better by thinking about the content as you read
Explanation	Good readers anticipate when they read. They think about what is coming next and try to guess what they will learn next.
Example	**Every year in July, Gilroy hosts the Garlic Festival. People from all over California and the United States come to attend this celebration of garlic.**
	Predictions
	The writer will explain what the garlic festival is.
	The writer will explain what people do at the festival.

Making Predictions

Read these sentences from the reading passage. Then make a prediction about what you will read.

1. "Where is the garlic?" This is a common question for visitors to Gilroy, California.

   ____

2. However, the most important and anticipated activity at the festival is the cook-off.

   ____

Skimming Practice

Skim the reading to find the main idea of each paragraph. Write the paragraph number next to the correct answer.

_____ The people of Gilroy are devoted to garlic.

_____ Gilroy is the leading producer of garlic products in the United States.

_____ The Garlic Festival in July is a popular event for tourists from all over the United States.

_____ Although Gilroy is called the Garlic Capital of the World, visitors don't see garlic when they enter the town.

_____ The garlic cook-off is the most anticipated activity at the festival.

Reading

The Garlic Capital of the World

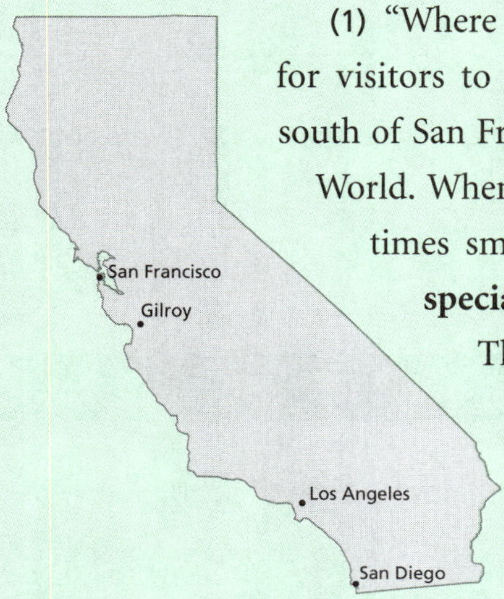

(1) "Where is the garlic?" This is a common question for visitors to Gilroy, California. Gilroy, about 75 miles south of San Francisco, calls itself the Garlic Capital of the World. When you drive through Gilroy, you can sometimes smell garlic, and you can see a lot of garlic **specialty** shops, but you can't see fields of garlic. There are some small garlic fields in Gilroy, but most of California's garlic comes from the San Joaquin Valley, east of Gilroy.

(2) So then, why is Gilroy the Capital of Garlic? It's because it is the leading producer of garlic products in the United States. In Gilroy, you can get pickled garlic, teriyaki garlic, hot mustard garlic, jalapeno garlic, and sweet and sour garlic. There is garlic wine and vinegar, garlic salt, and garlic salsa. Perhaps the most unusual garlic product is garlic ice cream!

(3) Every year in July, Gilroy **hosts** the Garlic Festival.* People from all over California and the United States come to attend this celebration of garlic. The first festival took place in 1979. It was held to **benefit** local charities and **non-profit** organizations. Nowadays, the festival still **benefit**s these groups, but it has grown considerably. More than 100,000 people come each year. At the festival, there are many kinds of activities, such as listening to bands and playing with your children in special "kids only" areas.

(4) However, the most important and **anticipated** activity at the festival is the garlic cook-off. A cook-off is a contest where people try to make the best garlic-themed food. Chefs and bakers **submit** recipes six months in advance. They hope that the judges will choose their recipe for presentation at the festival. Then, on Saturday afternoon, the winner is announced. He or she

*__festival__—*n.* a community celebration

receives a crown of garlic and $1,000. Past winning recipes have included spicy garlic butter cookies, walnut garlic tart, and garlic seafood soup.

(5) In short, while Gilroy doesn't have a lot of fields of garlic, it seems that it is indeed the Garlic Capital of the World. The people of Gilroy celebrate garlic by making unusual products, by sponsoring** a huge festival, and by **demonstrating devotion** to the taste and cuisine*** of garlic.

****sponsor**—*v.* help by giving money
*****cuisine**—*n.* a special type of cooking

Reading Comprehension

Circle the letter of the correct answer, or write a short answer.

1. Why is Gilroy called the Garlic Capital of the World?
   a. It always smells like garlic.
   b. There are a lot of fields of garlic.
   c. It produces more garlic products than any other place in the U.S.

2. How many garlic products does the article mention?
   a. 5
   b. 9
   c. 10

3. How long has there been a Garlic Festival in Gilroy?
   a. since 1979
   b. for 20 years
   c. for 60 years

4. What was the purpose of the first Garlic Festival?
   a. to raise money for charities
   b. to celebrate garlic
   c. to show local bands

5. How many people attend the Garlic festival every year?
   a. ten thousand
   b. one hundred thousand
   c. one thousand

6. The most popular activity at the Garlic Festival is the cook-off.
   a. true
   b. false
   c. The reading doesn't say.

7. Which recipe has won a prize at the Garlic Festival?
   a. garlic cookies
   b. garlic ice cream
   c. garlic pickles

8. What does the winner of the cook-off receive? ______________________________

   ____

9. People in Gilroy are proud of their devotion to garlic.
   a. true
   b. false
   c. The reading doesn't say.

Discuss Your Ideas

In small groups, discuss the answers to these questions. Be prepared to share your answers with the class.

1. Do people in your home country use garlic? Do you like garlic?
2. Is your hometown famous for a particular type of food or recipe? If so, what is it?
3. Would you like to participate in a cook-off? What kind of food would you cook?

Vocabulary Comprehension

With a classmate, fill in the empty boxes in the chart. Do not write anything in the boxes that have an X. You can use an English dictionary.

Nouns	Verbs	Adjectives	Adverbs
	anticipate		X
	benefit		X
	demonstrate		X
devotion			X
	host	X	X
	X	non-profit	X
specialty	X		X
	submit	X	X

STUDY TIP

Using the Internet: Some Cautions

The Internet is a wonderful source of information, but you need to be careful when using it. Here are some tips.

1. Not everything you read on the Internet is true. You need to verify the information you find. A good way to do this is to find the information in more than one site and to check out both sites.
2. To make sure that a website is has truthful information, look for a posting date, an author, and an institution connected with the site. Missing one of these doesn't automatically indicate that the information is questionable, but missing all three does.
3. Pay attention to the domain. Sites that use .edu are associated with universities and colleges and are generally good. Sites with .gov are associated with the government and are usually a good source for statistics, but, you need to evaluate the government itself and decide whether or not to trust it. Sites with .org are usually associated with non-profit organizations, whose information may be biased. Sites with .com are associated with businesses, and their information may be biased as well.

Matching

Match each word in the left column with its opposite in the right column.

____	1. anticipate	a. not expect
____	2. benefit	b. hatred
____	3. demonstrate	c. hide
____	4. devotion	d. hurt
____	5. host (n.)	e. keep
____	6. non-profit	f. guest
____	7. submit	g. money-making

Word Forms

Read the sentences. Change the incorrect word form in bold to the correct form.

_______________ 1. Children often **beneficial** from having a brother or sister.

_______________ 2. The teacher said that all of her students **submission** their homework on time.

_______________ 3. The surprise quiz clearly **demonstration** which students had read the homework assignment and which students had not.

_______________ 4. When I was a child, I was full of **anticipate** the day before my birthday.

_______________ 5. We **devotion** every weekday evening to helping our children with their homework.

Vocabulary Use

Vocabulary Note

Some of the target vocabulary in Chapter 9 has usages and meanings different that are from how they were used in the reading. To become a better reader, make sure you understand these phrase/usages:

benefit *to hold a benefit for* (an event to help support a non-profit)

demonstrate *to demonstrate responsibility* (show), *a demonstration* (protest)

True or False

Write T if the statement is true and F if the statement is false.

_____ 1. Non-profit organizations usually make a lot of money for their owners.

_____ 2. Brushing your teeth twice a day is beneficial for your health.

_____ 3. The baker's specialty is cooking meat.

_____ 4. The host locks the door when people arrive.

_____ 5. I didn't anticipate her visit, so I was surprised.

Write about It

Write a paragraph in response to the prompt. Try to use three words from the chart on page 111.

Compare and contrast life in a big city with life in a small town. How is it similar? How is it different?

CHAPTER

10

Loveland, Colorado

Getting Ready to Read

Discuss the questions with a classmate.

1. Have you ever been to Colorado? What have you heard about this state?
2. One town in Colorado is named Loveland. Why do you think the town has this name? Check one of these answers:
   a. It's a romantic town.
   b. Many people get married there.
   c. It's named after a famous person in the state.
3. What do you think of when you hear the name Loveland? How do you imagine this town?

Vocabulary Preview

For each sentence, choose one of the words or phrases to match the meaning of the word in bold.

being nice	non-paid worker
communication	not reserved yet
due date	question
marked in a special way	speaks or takes action for others

1. Two seats are **available** on the next flight to Colorado. Would you like to go?

   I think **available** means ____.

2. The boss gave us a **deadline** for finishing our work. We must finish everything by next Friday.

   I think **deadline** means ____.

3. I will never forget the **kindness** of my grandmother. She always treated me with love.

   I think **kindness** means ____.

4. One of the fastest ways to send a **message** to someone is by email. This is why so many people use email so much.

   I think **message** means ____.

5. The president of the United States **represents** the people of the U.S. Similarly, the president of Chile **represents** the people of Chile.

   I think **represents** means ____.

6. When you travel to a new country, you need to get your passport **stamped**. This shows that you have entered the country.

   I think **stamped** means ____.

7. Before my mother became a nurse, she worked as a **volunteer** in a hospital. She did this to learn more about hospital work.

   I think **volunteer** means ____.

8. I **wonder** how long it takes to fly from New York to Colorado. Does it take three or four hours?

   I think **wonder** means ____.

Reading Skill

Skill **Understanding Compound Sentences with Coordinating Conjunctions**

Purpose To understand the connection between sentences joined by coordinating conjunctions

Explanation Coordinating conjunctions, such as *and*, *or*, *but*, and *so*, combine two independent clauses to make compound sentences. The relationship between the two independent clauses changes depending on the coordinating conjunction.

- *and* = addition
- *so* = result
- *but* = contrast
- *or* = choice

Examples William Loveland founded the town,

- *and* he named it after himself.
- *but* he left shortly afterward.
- *so* he became the first mayor.
- *or* he founded the neighboring town.

Using Conjunctions

Read the sentences. Insert the coordinating conjunction. Then indicate the relationship (addition, contrast, result, choice) between the two independent clauses.

1. The state of Colorado has a town named Loveland, ______ most people don't know where the name comes from.

   ____

2. Many lovers want to find a special way to share their Valentine messages, ______ they mail their letters and cards to Loveland, Colorado.

   ____

3. There, the letters and cards are stamped with the Loveland postmark, ______ then they are re-mailed to all 50 states and more than 110 countries.

   ____

4. Post office workers can't deal with all the mail, ______ volunteers work in the remailing program.

   ____

5. They also wanted to help local businesses, ______ they thought the program would promote the town of Loveland and make it better known.

   ____

6. You can send a Valentine message from Loveland by mail, ______ you can do it online.

   ____

Reading

Sent with Love from Loveland, Colorado

The state of Colorado has a town named Loveland, but most people don't know where the name comes from. Some people **wonder** if it is a special place to fall in love. Others think it might be a peaceful place where people treat each other with **kindness.** Actually, the reason is simple. The town was founded in 1877 and named after William A.H. Loveland. He was the president of the Colorado Central Railroad and an important person in Colorado history. Today his name continues in this beautiful town of artists.

However, the main reason Loveland is famous today is the "Loveland Valentine Remailing Program." Each year on Valentine's Day (February 14), millions of Americans send cards and letters to their loved ones. Many lovers want to find a special way to do this, so they mail their Valentine **messages** to Loveland, Colorado. There, the letters and cards are **stamped** with the Loveland postmark,* and then they are remailed to all 50 states and more than 110 countries. Post office workers can't deal with all the mail, so **volunteers** work in the remailing program. One of them is "Miss Loveland Valentine," a high school student who is chosen each year to **represent** Loveland as she travels around the state and speaks in public.

The Loveland Valentine Remailing Program was founded more than 60 years ago by a happy couple from Loveland, Ted and Mabel Thompson. They wanted to share their town's name with lovers everywhere. They also wanted to help local businesses, and they thought the program would benefit the town of Loveland and make it better known.

***postmark**—*n.* an official mark that shows the date and place of mailing

You can send a Valentine **message** from Loveland by mail, or you can do it online. If you want to send a Valentine card from Loveland, put your **stamped** card or letter into a larger envelope. Then mail it to Postmaster, Attention Valentines, 446 E. 29th St., Loveland, CO 80538-9998. The **deadline** for international remailings is February 4, and the **deadline** for remailings within the United States is February 9.

The other way to send a Valentine **message** from Loveland is to order a card from the Loveland website. A special card is designed each year. You can order one or more of these cards online and send them from Loveland to anywhere in the world. More than a dozen different kinds of Valentine e-cards are **available** on the website. These e-cards include beautiful pictures of Colorado as well as pictures of sculptures from Loveland's famous sculpture** garden. You can write your own **message** and email these cards to your loved ones for free.

Happy Valentine's Day from Loveland, Colorado!

****sculpture**—*n.* a work of art made with wood, stone, or another hard material

Reading Comprehension

Circle the letter of the correct answer, or write a short answer.

1. No one knows exactly where the name Loveland came from.
   a. true
   b. false
   c. The reading doesn't say.

2. What is the main reason why people send their Valentine cards and letters to Loveland? ______________________________

   ____

3. The Loveland Valentine Remailing Program sends cards and letters internationally.
   a. true
   b. false
   c. The reading doesn't say.
4. Who is one of the most well-known volunteers each year?

   ____

5. Who did Ted and Mabel Thompson want to help?
   a. lovers
   b. local business owners
   c. both a and b
6. The deadline for international remailing is later than the deadline for remailing within the United States.
   a. true
   b. false
   c. The reading doesn't say.
7. There is only one way to send a Valentine message from Loveland.
   a. true
   b. false
   c. The reading doesn't say.
8. The Loveland website includes photographs from around the world.
   a. true
   b. false
   c. The reading doesn't say.
9. What special kind of art does the Loveland website promote? ________________

   ____

Discuss Your Ideas

In small groups, discuss the answers to these questions. Be prepared to share your answers with the class.

1. Do you know what Valentine's Day is? What do you know about it?
2. Why do you think volunteers want to work in the Loveland Valentine Remailing Program?
3. What are some other towns or cities that are named after important people?

STUDY TIP

Self-Editing: Using Commas

Good writers check their work carefully, including their use of commas. You should self-edit, especially when using coordinating conjunctions or lists. With a coordinating conjunction (*and, but, so, or*):

- Be sure to use a comma before the coordinating conjunction when joining two independent clauses.
- When joining three or four words together in a list, put a comma after each word in the list.

Vocabulary Comprehension

With a classmate, fill in the empty boxes in the chart. Do not write anything in the boxes that have an X. You can use an English dictionary.

Nouns	Verbs	Adjectives	Adverbs
	X	available	X
deadline	X	X	X
kindness	X		
message		X	X
1. 2.	represent		X
		stamped	X
volunteer			X
	wonder		

Sentence Completion

Fill in each blank with one of the words from the chart. Use the context to help you choose the correct form of the word. You may need to use a plural form.

1. You cannot apply for the job if you miss the application ____________________.
2. The school is looking for a ____________________ to help in the library.
3. I'm going to use the Internet to check the ____________________ of concert tickets. I hope that some good seats are left.
4. In the United States, people in each state vote for several ____________________ to speak and act for them in the government.
5. I have several ____________________ on my cell phone. I need to check to see who called.
6. Children often ____________________ about basic things, such as why the sky is blue.

7. When I visited Tokyo, I got lost. Because of the ____________________ of strangers, I got everywhere I needed to be.

8. My letter was returned to me. The Post Office will not deliver letters without ____________________.

Odd One Out

Circle the word that does not belong in each group. Be prepared to explain why the word does not belong.

1. available, ready, valuable, nearby
2. limit, due date, deadline, lawsuit
3. cruel, mean, kind, harsh
4. communication, message, content, style
5. representative, agent, enemy, spokesperson
6. banker, doctor, lawyer, volunteer
7. know, wonder, guess, speculate

Vocabulary Use

Vocabulary Note

Some of the target vocabulary in Chapter 10 has usages and meanings that are different from how they were used in the reading. To become a better reader, make sure you understand these phrase/usages:

represent *a representative sample; the House of Representatives*

wonder *a sense of wonder; no wonder*

Short Answer

Write an answer to these questions. Try to use the word in bold in your answer.

1. What kind of **stamps** do people collect? ______________________________

2. In the Olympics, who do the athletes **represent**? ______________________________

3. How can people check the **availability** of jobs? ______________________________

____

4. Why do we think of **volunteers** as generous people? ______________________________

5. What kind of **messages** can people leave with a cell phone? ______________________

____

Write about It

Write a paragraph in response to the prompt. Try to use at least three of the words from the chart on page 122 in this assignment.

You work in the office of tourism for Loveland. Your job and your goal is to make people want to visit Loveland. Write your description of the town for the tourism website.

Vocabulary Skill

Skill	**Recognizing Compound Nouns**
Purpose	To increase your understanding of words
Explanation	Compound nouns are formed when a noun combines with another word to make a new word. Compound nouns can be written as one word.
Examples	1. *sea* (ocean) + *food* (what you eat) = ***seafood*** (fish or other sea animals that you can eat) 2. *news* (what happens) + *paper* (something you write on) = ***newspaper*** (a piece of paper that has the news on it) 3. *tea* (something you make a drink from) + *cup* (something you drink from) = ***teacup*** (something you drink tea from)

Create Compound Nouns

Match one word from the left column with one word from the right column to make a compound noun.

1. air	book	____________________
2. day	end	____________________
3. home	light	____________________
4. life	mark	____________________
5. news	mate	____________________
6. post	paper	____________________
7. rail	port	____________________
8. team	road	____________________
9. text	span	____________________
10. week	town	____________________

Timed Reading

Read the passage according to your teacher's instructions. Then answer the questions on page 213 without looking at the reading.

The Most Remote Music Festival in the World

For centuries, the Touareg nomads of Northwest Africa have gathered once a year. They come to settle differences, to reconnect with each other, and to celebrate with music and dance. Since 2001, this meeting has expanded into the most remote music festival in the world. It is called the Festival of the Desert and takes place every January. In addition to the nomads, musicians from all over the world come together for three days to play music for each other. During these three days, African culture meets Western culture, and ancient rhythms meet electric guitars.

* The Festival in the Desert takes place in Essakane, Mali. This small village is located in the southern Sahara Desert near Timbuktu. It is a remote place where about 200 people live. It is a place of sand dunes and sand storms. There is not much to do during most of the year, so the festival is an exciting time for the people of Essakane. Since there are no buildings in Essakane, people set up big tents when they arrive for the festival. Musicians and festival attendees eat, sleep, and play under these tents. During the hot day, people lis- * ten to traditional Touareg music and poetry and watch dances and camel races. At night, the air gets cold, and the stars come out. This is when the Festival of the Desert really starts. Musicians from Africa, Asia, Australia, and Europe play their music late into the night.

The Festival of the Desert has brought international attention to the Touareg people. Their nomadic lives have not been easy, and their music and songs reflect their difficulties. It can be soulful and sad. The Touareg people are sometimes called the blue people because the blue dye of their robes stays on their skin. This seems like a good name for musicians who play desert blues. Touareg music can also reflect the anger and frustration of young people who feel like there is no place in the world for them. Tinariwen is a popular Touareg band which has gained international popularity. The members of Tinariwen play their electric guitars at full volume and sing of pain, unemployment, and exile.

The Touareg people are proud of their Festival of the Desert, the most remote music festival in the world. They hope to host it for many years. Most festival attendees agree that it is an amazing experience.

UNIT 6

Americana

Americana includes any kind of object (toy, hat, food, and so on) that is closely related to American culture. It can also include a game or activity that seems typically American.

Discuss these questions in small groups.

1. Which country are you from? What makes you proud of your country?
2. How do people show how they feel about their country? Give examples.
3. Look at the list. Place a check mark (✓) next to the items that seem to be Americana.

____ a baseball bat

____ a soccer ball

____ apple pie

____ sushi

____ an eagle

____ a panda bear

____ a cowboy hat

____ mountain climbing

CHAPTER

11

Spelling Bees

Getting Ready to Read

Work with a partner. One of you will be Student A, and the other will be Student B. Sit so you aren't facing each other, and use a piece of paper to cover your classmate's part of the chart. Follow the instructions.

Student A	Student B
Part 1	Part 1
Say these words to your partner.	*Spell the words that your partner says.*
1. believe	1. ______________________
2. eight	2. ______________________
3. quite	3. ______________________
4. bought	4. ______________________
5. through	5. ______________________

Student A	Student B
Part 2 *Write the words that your partner says.* 1. ______ 2. ______ 3. ______ 4. ______ 5. ______	Part 2 *Say these words to your partner.* 1. enough 2. foreign 3. late 4. piece 5. thought

Check your answers with your partner. How well did you do?

Vocabulary Preview

For each sentence, choose one of the words or phrases to match the meaning of the word in bold.

a lot	stopped
collected together	took a strong position
first	urged
similar	useful

1. English Breakfast tea and Earl Grey tea are **alike**. They are black teas with strong flavors.

   I think **alike** means ______________________.

2. The storm **ceased** other serveral hours, making it possible for the clear up to begin.

   I think **ceased** means ______________________.

3. Sandy moved to Washington, DC, for her new job. The job was very stressful, so she quit and moved back to Denver. Then, she was **considerably** more relaxed.

   I think **considerably** means ______________________.

4. I like the new person on our team, but he has **dominated** the conversation in all of our meetings.

   I think **dominated** means ______________________________.

5. Bobby was a bad speller in fourth grade, but his parents and his teacher **encouraged** him to study more. After that, he got better.

   I think **encouraged** means ______________________________.

6. I grew up on a farm, and every fall my brothers and I **gathered** all the apples that fell to the ground. We had to pick them up and put them in a big basket.

   I think **gathered** means ______________________________.

7. The **original** spelling of my last name was Andriç, but my grandfather changed it to Andrich so that people would pronounce it correctly.

   I think **original** means ______________________________.

8. An explorer in the Arctic or the Antarctic usually wears a bright color like red. Red is used for **practical** reasons. People need to be able to see each other against the white background of the snow and ice.

   I think **practical** means ______________________________.

Reading Skill

Skill	**Making Inferences**
Purpose	To understand important information that is not stated directly in the text
Example	**When I first saw the house, it was covered with snow, and there was smoke coming from the chimney.**
Explanation	Indirectly, the author is saying that there is a fireplace in the house and that there is a fire burning there. How do you know that? There was a fire because there was smoke coming from the chimney. When you understand something that the author doesn't say directly, you are **making an inference**.

Making Inferences

Look at the sample sentences from the reading. Each sentence is followed by two statements. One is a correct inference, and the other is not. With a classmate, decide which one is the inference. Be prepared to explain your answers.

1. English has 44 sounds, but there are only 26 letters, so some letters have to do double or triple the work.
   a. Some letters have more than one sound.
   b. Eighteen letters represent more than one sound.
2. The contest was called a spelling bee. The word *bee* in this case means a social gathering.
   a. *Bee* has more than one meaning in English.
   b. A social gathering is called a *bee.*
3. Some people say that the difficult spelling in English shouldn't be celebrated with spelling bees.
   a. Not everyone thinks spelling bees are a good idea.
   b. Spelling bees are happy occasions.
4. Even so, it's hard to believe that spelling bees would cease to exist.
   a. Popular events cease to exist.
   b. Spelling bees are very popular.

Scanning Practice

Scan the reading for the answers to these questions.

1. What country dominated England? ____________________
2. When did the first spelling bee occur? ____________________
3. Who won it? ____________________
4. How much money did he win? ____________________

Spelling Bees

Students of English already know how difficult spelling in English is. When do you use *ie*? When do you use *ei*? Why is *e* sometimes silent? And why don't the words *rough*, *dough*, and *cough* sound **alike**?

English spelling is difficult for historical and **practical** reasons. Historically, France **dominated** England for several hundred years, so many French words became part of English. Many Greek and Latin words were added later. These languages were considered better than English, so the **original** spelling was kept. The **practical** reason is that English has 44 sounds, but there are only 26 letters, so some letters have to do double or triple the work. For example, *c* is one letter with two pronunciations: *k* (*cup*) and *s* (*city*).

Learning these spelling rules has been difficult and boring for students for many, many years. In 1925, a newspaper in Louisville, Kentucky, decided to hold a contest to find the best speller in the country. The people at the newspaper wanted to **encourage** students to become good spellers and to learn a lot of words. The contest was called a Spelling Bee. The word *bee* in this case means a social **gathering**.

In 1925, nine students competed for a prize* of $500 and a chance to meet the president of the United States, Calvin Coolidge. The winner was Frank Neuhauser. He won by spelling the word *gladiolus* correctly. Since then, there have been more than 80 national spelling bees. The biggest is called the Scripps National Spelling Bee, and it has been broadcast on TV since 2006. In 2009, there were 293 contestants. The winner was Kavya Shivashanker from Kansas. He won by spelling the word *Laodicean* correctly. His prize was **considerably** bigger than Frank Neuhauser's. He won more than $35,000 in cash and scholarship money.

The spelling bee has become part of the culture of the United States, but not everyone thinks spelling bees are good ideas. Some people say that the difficult spelling in English shouldn't be celebrated. Some say that the rules of English spelling should change so that it is easier to spell in English. Even so, it's hard to believe that spelling bees would **cease** to exist. They are much too popular. And they make learning English spelling a little more interesting.

Reading Comprehension

Circle the letter of the correct answer, or write a short answer.

1. Which country dominated English in historic times?
   a. France
   b. Greece
   c. Rome
2. Who was the U.S. president in 1925? ______________________________
3. How many more students competed in the 2009 spelling bee than in the 1925 spelling bee? ______________________________
4. There has been a national spelling bee contest every year since 1925.
   a. true
   b. false
   c. The reading doesn't say.
5. Which of the following statements is NOT true?
   a. Spelling bees are popular.
   b. Spelling bees make spelling interesting.
   c. Spelling bees may cease to exist.

6. In 1925, Kavya Shivashanker won the spelling bee by spelling the word *Laodicean* correctly.
   a. true
   b. false
   c. The reading doesn't say.
7. Spelling bees are sometimes broadcast on the radio.
   a. true
   b. false
   c. The reading doesn't say.
8. What is a sewing bee?
   a. a kind of insect
   b. a gathering where everyone sews
   c. a social gathering

Discuss Your Ideas

In small groups, discuss the answers to these questions. Be prepared to share your answers with the class.

1. Do you have problems with spelling in English? Which English words are difficult for you to spell?
2. Do you know any spelling rules for English? If so, share them with your group.
3. Give three reasons why the newspaper in Louisville decided to have a spelling contest. Which do you think was the primary reason? Why?
4. Do you think spelling bees are a good idea? Why or why not?

STUDY TIP

Reducing Test Anxiety

Do your best to prepare for a test by giving yourself time to study. Don't try to learn everything the night before the test. Get plenty of sleep, and be sure to arrive a few minutes early for the test. Remember that you don't have to get every answer right to get a good score.

Vocabulary Comprehension

With a classmate, fill in the empty boxes in the chart. Do not write anything in the boxes that have an X. You can use an English dictionary.

Nouns	Verbs	Adjectives	Adverbs
X	X	alike	X
	cease		X
X	X		considerably
	dominate	X	X
	encourage		X
	gather	X	X
1. 2.		original	X
X	practical		

Matching

Match each word in the left column with its opposite meaning in the right column.

____	1. alike	a. continue
____	2. cease	b. less
____	3. considerable	c. different
____	4. dominate	d. prevent
____	5. encourage	e. submit to
____	6. gather	f. hand out
____	7. practical	g. useless

Word Forms

Fill in each blank with the correct form of the word in bold.

1. **encouragement, encourage**

   The skater won the gold medal with the _______________ of her parents, her coaches, and her teammates.

2. **gathering, gathers**

   Before she leaves for work, Kate ________________ the things she needs for the day: her briefcase, her gym bag, her purse, and her coffee.

3. **origin, original, originally**

   Carlos is _________________ from Spain. He now lives in Chicago.

4. **considerable, considerably**

   My new job pays ___________________ more than my old job. Now, I have enough money to buy a new car.

5. **practical, practically**

   The wheel is one of the most ________________ inventions of all time. It has been used in nearly every aspect of life since its invention more than 5,000 years ago.

Vocabulary Use

Vocabulary Note

Some of the target vocabulary in Chapter 11 has usages and meanings that are different from how they were used in the reading. To become a better reader, make sure you understand these phrase/usages:

cease *a cease fire* (stop firing weapons); *to cease to exist*

dominate *to dominate the opposing team*; *to dominate the conversation*

True or False

Write T if the statement is true and F if the statement is false.

____ 1. An art specialist can tell if a painting is the original or a copy.

____ 2. You should encourage obese people to eat more.

____ 3. Some countries dominate much of the oil supply.

____ 4. Wearing a rain coat when it is raining is a practical idea.

____ 5. Apples and bananas look alike.

____ 6. It is considerably colder in Hawaii than it is in Alaska.

Write about It

Write a paragraph in response to the prompt. Try to use three words from the chart on page 137.

An artifact is something made or used by people of a culture. Artifacts include food, clothing, toys, musical instruments, jewelry, and technological devices. Which artifact best represents your home culture? Why?

CHAPTER

12

Teddy Bear Mania

Getting Ready to Read

There are many kinds of toys. One popular toy in the United States is the teddy bear. Some people even dress the bears in special clothing. For example, their bears may be dressed like cowboys or ballerinas. Discuss these questions with a classmate.

1. What kind of toys have you played with? Have you ever owned a teddy bear?
2. Are teddy bears popular in your culture?
3. What are some other popular toys?

Vocabulary Preview

For each sentence, choose one of the words to match the meaning of the word in bold.

a completed goal or task	planned in a special way
established	related to money
focused	set of steps
not too proud	types

1. The teddy bear was **created** in honor of President Theodore Roosevelt, who lived from 1858–1919.

   I think **created** means ____.

2. This toy was **designed** for children to play with and enjoy.

   I think **designed** means ____.

3. Today, there are many different **styles** of teddy bear. Some are fancy with many pretty clothes, and others have only a bow around their necks.

   I think **styles** means ____.

4. The teddy bear business has brought some people **financial** success. In fact, selling teddy bears is a big business in many countries.

   I think **financial** means ____.

5. My friend has made a lot of money in business, but she never talks about it because she is very **modest.**

   I think **modest** means ____.

6. People will often say *congratulations* when they hear about a special achievement.

   I think **achievement** means ____.

7. The test **emphasized** the material in the last two chapters of our textbook.

   I think **emphasized** means ____.

8. Children in all countries learn their first languages by the same **process**.

   I think **process** means ____.

Reading Skill

Skill	**Understanding Pronoun Reference**
Purpose	To understand that pronouns refer to other words in a text
Definitions	1. Personal pronouns include: *him, her, them, it.*
	2. Demonstrative pronouns include: *this, that, these, those.*
	3. Indefinite pronouns include: *all, any, many, one.*
Examples	1. **Helen loves her *teddy bear,* and always plays with *it.***
	it = teddy bear
	2. **If you want to buy some toys, please look at *these.***
	these = toys
	3. **The boys didn't like the old toy and wanted a new *one.***
	one = toy

Understanding Pronoun Reference

Read each set of sentences. Circle the pronoun in the second sentence in each set. Underline the word that it refers to in the first sentence.

1. a. As a little girl, teddy bears were Maxine Clark's favorite toys.
   b. These were also loved by millions of other American children.

2. a. Maxine was shopping for toys with the 10-year-old daughter of a friend.
   b. The little girl suggested making them instead of buying them.

3. a. Other children gave Maxine advice on how to dress a teddy bear.
   b. They also gave advice on the process of building one.

Reading

Build-A-Bear® Workshop

Can you remember your favorite toy, the one that you loved the most? When Maxine Clark was a little girl, her favorite toy was a teddy bear. Millions of other American children also loved and still love teddy bears. Teddy bears first appeared in 1902, when a bear toy was **created** in honor of President Theodore "Teddy" Roosevelt. Like other **creative** thinkers, Maxine Clark found a way to share something that was important to her with many other people.

In 1996, Maxine was shopping for toys with the 10-year-old daughter of a friend. When the little girl suggested making the toys instead of buying them, Maxine realized that she could make and sell teddy bears as a business. Together with her young partner, she **designed** several types of bears. She thought that it might be better to sell the bears without names so that the buyers could choose their own name for the bears. This small production was the beginning of Build-A-Bear Workshop, now a world-famous toy company. Maxine learned to accept the advice of groups of children on everything from how to dress a teddy bear to ways to make the **process** of building a bear more fun.

Today, children and adults in more than 15 countries enjoy making themselves a "beary" good friend. First, they choose an animal, such as a bear, pony, monkey, cat, or dog. Next, they choose a voice and recorded message for the toy animal to "speak." After that, they stuff* the toy animal and place a toy heart inside it. Finally, they **create** a special look for the toy by putting clothes

*__stuff__—*v.* to fill with a soft material

on it. They can also add sunglasses, jewelry, or anything else. They can choose from many different **styles.**

Maxine has experienced great **financial** success as a result of Build-A-Bear Workshop. Still, she is **modest** when she describes her **achievement**. She remembers the advice of a business professor who taught her in college. He **emphasized** the importance of selling a product in a new and exciting way. Maxine admits** that she did not invent the teddy bear. It was already a treasured American toy. Her new and exciting idea was to allow people to **create** their own special bear. As she listened to children, she **designed** her business and found success.

****admit**—*v.* to agree that something is true

Reading Comprehension

Circle the letter of the correct answer or write a short answer.

1. Who invented the teddy bear?
   a. Maxine Clark
   b. Theodore Roosevelt
   c. The reading doesn't say.
2. Which phrase best describes Maxine Clark?
   a. a person with a creative idea
   b. a person who admired the President
   c. a person who collected teddy bears
3. Where did Maxine get her business idea from
   a. a workshop
   b. a friend.
   c. a child.

4. Children can only make teddy bears at Build-a-Bear Workshop.
   a. true
   b. false
   c. The reading doesn't say.

5. Which phrase best describes Build-A-Bear Workshop?
   c. a toy company with stores in more than a dozen countries
   b. an American toy company that sells stuffed animals
   c. a famous company that designs and sells teddy bears

6. How many steps does it take to build a toy animal?
   a. 2–3
   b. 4–5
   c. 5–7

7. What was Maxine's most important lesson at business school?
   a. try to invent something new
   b. try to achieve financial success
   c. try to sell something in a new way

8. Maxine got some of her best ideas from other business people.
   a. true
   b. false
   c. The reading doesn't say.

Discuss Your Ideas

In small groups, discuss the answers to these questions. Be prepared to share your answers with the class.

1. Would you enjoy building your own stuffed toy? What kind would you build?
2. What kind of recorded messages would you place inside a teddy bear?
3. Why do you think Maxine listened so carefully to children?
4. Try to think of a "new and exciting" way to sell a common product like pencils, yogurt, or bicycles.

STUDY TIP

Test-Taking Techniques

There are several things to do before you begin a test.

- Look over the entire test.
- Decide which section you will do first. Some students like to answer the easier questions first in order to build their confidence.
- Note the point value given to each section of the test. Spend more time on the parts of the test that have the highest point value.
- Plan your time.

Remember two things after you start the test.

- Keep track of time.
- Ask if you don't understand something.

Vocabulary Comprehension

With a classmate, fill in the empty boxes in the chart. Do not write anything in the boxes that have an X. You can use an English dictionary.

Nouns	Verbs	Adjectives	Adverbs
achievement		X	X
1. 2.	create		
1. 2.	design	X	X
	emphasize		
		financial	
	X	modest	
process			X
style	X		

Sentence Completion

Fill in each blank with one of the words from the chart. Use the context to help you choose the correct form of the word.

1. At Build-A-Bear workshop, you can become a teddy bear ______________ as you decide what your teddy bear will look like.
2. Some people dress their teddy bears very ______________ in the latest fashions.
3. Building a bear is a ______________ that includes several steps: choosing a bear, recording a message, stuffing the bear, and choosing clothes. Since you are making the bear from nothing, it is a very ______________ activity.
4. In the final step of building a bear, you choose clothing to ______________ whatever you like: a sport, a hobby, or a special kind of job. That way, the bear shows what you think is important.

5. Maxine's business idea has been very successful. Her ______________ has made her proud of her work even if her ______________ keeps her from telling a lot of people.

6. Build-a-Bear Workshop has helped Maxine ______________. She can now buy anything she wants!

Odd One Out

Circle the word that does not belong in each group. Be prepared to explain why the word does not belong.

1. achieve, effort, succeed, accomplish
2. improve, make, create, produce
3. emphasize, stress, draw attention, realize
4. final, monetary, financial, economic
5. proud, humble, modest, shy
6. stage, result, step, process
7. style, way, manner, selection
8. design, plan, increase, construct

Vocabulary Use

Vocabulary Note

Some of the target vocabulary in Chapter 12 has usages and meanings that are different from how they were used in the reading. To become a better reader, make sure you understand these phrase/usages:

process *in the process of; to process a claim*

Short Answer

Write an answer to the questions. Try to use the bold word in your answer.

1. What kind of **design** should a house have for tropical weather?

____

2. What should people do to take care of themselves **financially**?

____

3. What subject do elementary school teachers **emphasize**?

____

4. Which job is more **creative:** a salesperson or a painter? Why?

____

Vocabulary Skill

Skill — **Learning Prefixes**

Purpose — To learn common prefixes and their meanings

Explanation — Prefixes come at the beginning of a word and change the meaning of the word.

Examples — Prefixes that mean "not"

de-	*code / decode*
dis-	*honest / dishonest*
im-	*possible / impossible*
in-	*finitely / infinitely*
ir-	*responsible/ irresponsible*
un-	*able / unable*

Other prefixes

inter-	(between)	*national / international*
pre-	(before)	*dawn / predawn*
re-	(again)	*use / reuse*
sub-	(under)	*human / subhuman*
super-	(over)	*market / supermarket*

Prefixes

Write one word from the box on page 149 in each blank. Some of the words that you choose will have prefixes.

1. It is ______________ for me to fly to Mexico. It is ______________ for me to fly to Mars.
2. In horror movies, some of the characters seem less than ______________. These ______________ creatures terrorize people in the movies—and in the audiences!
3. My favorite time of day is the ______________ hour before the sun comes up. It's always so quiet and peaceful. After ______________, my family gets up and starts making noise.
4. Some people are ______________ at least sometimes. It seems they can't always tell the truth.
5. The ______________ weather report was full of natural disasters. There was an earthquake in South America, a hurricane in North America, and a tsunami off the coast of Asia.
6. When you need a lot of supplies, it's better to go to a ______________ than to a local ______________. At the bigger store, things are usually much cheaper.

Write about It

Write a paragraph of response to the prompt. Try to use at least three of the words from the chart on page 147 in this assignment.

The idea for an American flag with 50 stars came from 17-year-old Robert Heft in 1958. (At first, his teacher told him it wasn't a very good idea!) Do you have any ideas for changing the design of the American flag or the flag of your home country? How would you change it?

Timed Reading

Read the passage according to your teacher's instructions. Then answer the questions on page 214 without looking at the reading.

America and Apple Pie

The phrase *as American as apple pie* is used to describe something as totally American. But why is apple pie considered so "American?" The truth is that apples are not native to North America, and neither are pies. Still, apple pies have become a big part of the culture in the United States.

The first settlers from England brought apples to the New World in the 1600s. However, when the apple trees started to produce apples, the colonists didn't use them to make pies. They were used to make cider. Later, apples
* spread west. In the early 1800s, John Chapman, a farmer from Massachusetts, walked through the Midwest planting apple seeds. His story became the legend of Johnny Appleseed. As most children in the United States know, Johnny Appleseed walked barefoot, wore a pan on his head, and planted apple trees across North America.

The first pies were probably made by the Greeks. The Romans took the idea from the Greeks and spread it to Europe. However, most pies at that time were meat pies. Moreover, the crusts were primarily used to keep the inside ingredients from spoiling. One pie recipe from England used apples,
* but the crust wasn't made for eating. Women in England began making fruit pies in the 1500s, so when colonists came to North America, the practice of pie making was well-known. As settlers spread across America, fruit pies became common.

In the 1800s, farming communities began having social gatherings called fairs. Each summer, farmers would gather to show off their animals and produce. At the fairs, judges chose the best example of any animal or piece of produce. Soon, women started displaying pies, and judges would determine the best-tasting pie. Naturally, apple pie was a favorite. This tradition of state * fairs became very American. In the last 100 years or so, another activity has become popular at state fairs: pie-eating contests. In these events, contestants try to eat more pies than any other contestant in a set period of time. The winner usually doesn't want to eat any more pie for a while but does enjoy having the cash prize.

In short, as it turns out, the apple pie is not really an American invention. Apples came from Europe, and so did the idea of a pie. However, like many ideas from other places, the apple pie has evolved to become part of the American culture.

UNIT 7

Car Racing

How much do you already know about cars?

With a classmate, discuss whether these statements are true or false. Check your answers at the bottom of the page.

1. The first engine was built more than 200 years ago.
2. At first, seat belts were offered as extra equipment.
3. Toyota was the first Japanese car company to produce cars in the United States.
4. Honda was the first company to sell hybrid gas/electric cars to consumers.
5. Speed limits were not enforced until the mid-1950s.
6. Per capita, China has the largest number of cars in the world.
7. The average household in the United States has three cars.
8. The first car race in the United States took place in 1895.

Answers: 1. T; 2. T; 3. F (It was Honda.); 4. T; 5. F (The first speeding ticket was given in 1902); 6. F (The United States has the largest.); 7. F (The average is 2.28.); 8. T (in Massachusetts)

CHAPTER

13

Online Instructions

Getting Ready to Read

Today it's possible to find out how to do almost anything by searching online. Professionals and amateurs write articles and blogs about how to do different things. Discuss these questions with a partner.

1. Do you know how to fix a car? What kinds of changes or repairs can you make to a car?
2. Would you enjoy building your own car? Why or why not?
3. Would you try to fix your car with online instructions? Why or why not?

Vocabulary Preview

For each sentence, choose one of the words or phrases to match the meaning of the word in bold.

buy	physical or mental power
completion	rules
group of similar things or people	the shape something is in
items needed for a purpose	time period

1. He wanted to join the army, but the doctor said he had a heart **condition.**

   I think **condition** means ______________________________.

2. The **fulfillment** of my childhood dream occurred the day I became a doctor.

   I think **fulfillment** means ______________________________.

3. Don't forget to bring your fishing **equipment** when you go to the river.

   I think **equipment** means ______________________________.

4. Most Americans borrow money from the bank when they **purchase** a car.

   I think **purchase** means ______________________________.

5. Bananas and grapes belong to the same **category** of food.

   I think **category** means ______________________________.

6. My grandmother was born before the **era** of cell phones and laptops.

   I think **era** means ______________________________.

7. Do you have the **energy** to run a marathon?

   I think **energy** means ______________________________.

8. The traveler was stopped because he did not meet the custom **regulations** for the U.S.

   I think **regulations** means ______________________________.

Reading Skill

Skill	**Distinguishing Fact from Opinion**
Purpose	To increase your understanding of a reading and recognize the writer's feelings
Explanation	*Facts* are pieces of true information. They are sometimes related to size, amount, or number. *Opinions* are what someone thinks. Other people can agree or disagree.
Examples	**Car racing is more than a hobby. It is the fulfillment of a dream.** **Car racing is a hobby.** (fact) **Car racing is the fulfillment of a dream.** (opinion)

Fact or Opinion?

Read these sentences from the reading. Then read the sentences that follow. Write F if it is a fact and O if it is an opinion.

1. Use the Internet to study the rules and regulations for all racing classes.
   ____ All racing classes have rules and regulations.
   ____ Some rules and regulations are too difficult to follow.

2. In the historical category, cars of a particular era are raced.
   ____ Cars from the 1920s era are the best cars.
   ____ Cars from the same era race against each other.

3. The lighter your car, the faster it will race.
   ____ A light car can go faster than a heavy car.
   ____ Keeping your car light is the most important part of racing.

4. Ask other racers about the best places to shop for car parts, equipment, and paint.
   ____ Some places are bad for shopping.
   ____ Other racers can share information with you.

Reading

How to Make Your Own Race Car

What if you could make your car go faster? Have you ever wanted to be in a car race? You might need a special car to be in a race. These are some simple steps to make a race car:

1. Count your money first. Don't make plans to make something you can't afford. Start with a clear idea of how much you are able to spend.
2. Use the Internet to study the rules and **regulations** for the different racing classes. Some of the different car classes include single-seater, off-road, sports car, and stock car. In the single-make **category**, cars from a single manufacturer, such as Honda or Ford, compete. In the historical **category,** cars of a particular **era** are raced.
3. Buy a car in good **condition**. Next, strip* the inside of your car according to the **regulations** of your racing class. The lighter your car, the faster it will race.
4. **Purchase** and put in all the racing **equipment** recommended by the **category** such as racing brakes** and safety belts. Focus on the most important **equipment** first, keeping your budget in mind. Save some money to hire a good mechanic who can help you find the power and speed you need to win the race.
5. Buy the best racing tires that you can afford. The better your tires, the faster your car will race.
6. Find a sponsor. Do you know any business owners? Tell them you will paint their company names and logos*** on the sides of your car. Then smile and ask them for some money to help pay for that car.

***strip**—*v.* remove unneeded parts
****brakes**—*n.* the part of a car that allows a driver to stop it
*****logo**—*n.* an image or word that represents the name of a company

7. Make friends with other racers. Ask them about the best places to shop for car parts, **equipment**, paint, and anything else you need or want. Ask for help, too. Don't try to do everything yourself—save some of your **energy** for Race Day.
8. Don't forget to put in a comfortable seat. When the big day comes, you'll want a smooth ride.

Here are some thoughts and advice from other racers:

> "This is more than a hobby. This is the **fulfillment** of a dream. Don't start racing unless you feel your life will be incomplete without it."
>
> —*Brian, Colorado*

> "I'm happy to have something I love to do and something that I'm good at doing."
>
> —*Josh, Nebraska*

> "If you think you might like racing your own car, start by looking at races online. Then take some racing lessons. Start going to races and talk to other people who love racing. Before long you'll know exactly what you want to do."
>
> —*Samantha, Ohio*

You've been dreaming long enough. Now it's time to get your engine started and race into the real world, the exciting world of fast cars and winning speed.

Reading Comprehension

Circle the letter of the correct answer, or write a short answer.

1. The purpose of this article is to
   a. give advice on making your own race car
   b. encourage readers to make their own race car
   c. a and b

2. In which category are cars of a particular era raced? ____________________

3. A sponsor is a business owner who will help pay for a race car in exchange for free advertising.
   a. true
   b. false
   c. The reading doesn't say.

4. Which driver recommends learning about racing step by step?
   a. Brian
   b. Josh
   c. Samantha

5. Which driver feels that racing completes his/her life?
   a. Brian
   b. Josh
   c. Samantha

6. Which phrase best describes people who like to make race cars?
   a. good mechanics
   b. independent and brave
   c. members of a community

7. A good race car should be fast and
   a. inexpensive
   b. attractive
   c. comfortable

8. According to the reading, racing a car takes a lot of
   a. energy
   b. courage
   c. patience

Discuss Your Ideas

In small groups, discuss the answers to these questions. Be prepared to share your answers with the class.

1. Does building a race car seem easy or difficult to you? Explain your answer.
2. Which category of race car interests you the most: single-make, historical, off-road, or sports car? Why?
3. Brian describes race car driving as "the fulfillment of a dream"? What kind of activity have you dreamed of doing? Have you taken any steps to fulfill this dream?

STUDY TIP

Understanding How a Text Is Organized

Good readers pay attention to how a text is organized or put together. They pay attention to titles and subtitles to identify main ideas. They also pay attention to the first sentence of each paragraph. This is usually the **topic sentence**, which contains the main idea of each paragraph. Good readers notice if the topic sentence is adding more information about a topic, or if it is introducing a new topic.

Vocabulary Comprehension

With a classmate, fill in the empty boxes in the chart. Do not write anything in the boxes that have an X. You can use an English dictionary.

Nouns	Verbs	Adjectives	Adverbs
category			
condition	X		
equipment			X
energy			
era	X	X	X
fulfillment		1. 2.	X
	purchase	X	X
regulation			X

Matching

Match each word in the left column with its opposite meanings in the right column.

____	1. energetic	a. not done
____	2. fulfill	b. sell
____	3. regulated	c. independent of
____	4. equipped	d. tired
____	5. purchase	e. individualize
____	6. conditional	f. uncontrolled
____	7. categorize	g. not ready

Word Forms

Read the sentences. Change the incorrect word form in bold to the correct form.

__________________ 1. Fruit and meat belong to different **categorical** of food.

__________________ 2. Race cars are **equipment** with special brakes.

__________________ 3. Eating nutritious food will **energetic** you.

__________________ 4. I want to **fulfillment** my dream of being an actor.

__________________ 5. What is the most important **regulated** in this race?

Vocabulary Use

Vocabulary Note

Some of the target vocabulary in Chapter 13 has usages and meanings that are different from how they were used in the reading. To become a better reader, make sure you understand these phrase/usages:

condition *to be in no condition [to do something]* (not able); *to be in critical condition; the conditions of a contract*

era *the golden era; a new era*

True or False

Write T if the statement is true and F if the statement is false.

____ 1. You can save money by purchasing a used car instead of a new one.

____ 2. Camping in the mountains does not require any equipment.

____ 3. Athletes have many techniques for keeping their bodies in good condition.

____ 4. Many people feel more energetic after drinking coffee.

____ 5. We can categorize people according to the languages they speak.

____ 6. A fulfilled dream is one that has come true.

____ 7. People have worn the same kinds of clothing in every era.

____ 8. Professional sports players do not have to follow regulations when they play.

Write about It

Write a paragraph in response to the prompt. Try to use at least three of the words from the chart on page 161.

Racing a car is a dangerous, even deadly, activity. Why do some people enjoy doing dangerous activities? What are the benefits?

CHAPTER

14

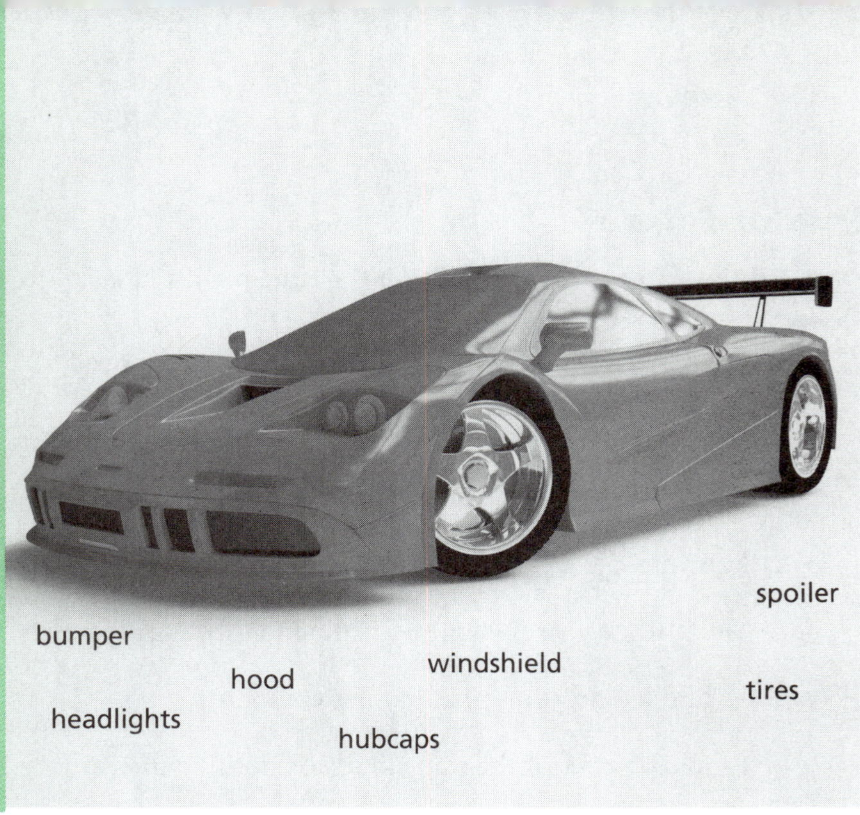

NASCAR

Getting Ready to Read

Do you know the names of parts of race cars? Some of the parts are the same as all cars. Others can only be found on race cars. With a classmate, draw an arrow from the name to the part on the car. Then discuss the questions.

1. How popular is car racing in your home culture?

2. Would you like to drive a race car? Why or why not?

Vocabulary Preview

For each sentence, choose one of the words or phrases to match the meaning of the word in bold.

co-workers	permission
in time	setting up
make someone think about something	value
a period of ten years	a way of living

1. When you need help, you **appreciate** anyone who can help you.

   I think **appreciate** means ____________________________________.

2. When you get a new job, it's a good idea to get to know some of your **colleagues**. They can help you learn about the organization.

   I think **colleagues** means ____________________________________.

3. My friends are trying to **convince** me to buy a new car. They say that my car is too old.

   I think **convince** means ____________________________________.

4. The **decade** between 1965 and 1975 brought many changes to the United States and its **culture.**

   I think **decade** means ____________________________________.

   I think **culture** means ____________________________________.

5. This is the location where the city is **establishing** a new elementary school for the children in the neighborhood. It will be ready in 18 months.

   I think **establishing** means ____________________________________.

6. **Eventually**, more than 250 students will attend this school.

   I think **eventually** means ______________________________.

7. Poets sometimes use language in unusual ways. This is called having poetic **license.**

   I think **license** means ______________________________.

Reading Skill

Skill	**Recognizing Transition Words**
Purpose	To understand the relationship between sentences
Explanation	Transition words connect two sentences. There are many of them in English, but a few of the most common are listed. Note that each transition has a meaning.

- **addition** — *additionally, furthermore*
- **conclusion** — *in short, in conclusion, in the end*
- **contrast** — *however, in contrast*
- **emphasis** — *in fact, indeed*
- **result** — *therefore, as a result*
- **time** — *first, next, then, finally*

Using Transitions

Complete each sentence on the left with the correct sentence on the right. Use the transition to help you choose the best answer.

____ 1. Some don't understand why car racing is popular. **However,**

____ 2. Car racing doesn't have a lot of rules. **Therefore,**

____ 3. Automobiles have a long history in the United States. **In fact,**

____ 4. The first stock car race took place in Daytona in 1936. **After that,**

____ 5. Bill France was a race car driver. **Furthermore,**

a. NASCAR was established.

b. he was the first president of NASCAR.

c. thousands of other people think it is exciting and watch it all the time.

d. it is easy for the whole family to understand it.

e. the first major U.S. car manufacturer opened in 1898.

Scanning Practice

Scan the reading for the answers to these questions.

1. What does NASCAR stand for? ________________________________
2. How many NASCAR races are there every year? ____________________
3. How many people go to NASCAR races every year? __________________
4. When did Daytona's first stock car race occur? _____________________
5. When was NASCAR established?________________________________

Reading

The National Association for Stock Car Racing

NASCAR racing is one of the most popular sports in the United States. Almost 100 races take place each year, and they are attended by more than 75 million fans. People who are not car racing fans can't understand why anyone would find watching car racing fun. However, many people in the United States love it, and it is the second most-watched sporting event on TV. So, why is it so popular?

One reason is that car racing doesn't require a natural athletic ability like most other sports do. Therefore, if you can drive a car, you can **appreciate** the skill of a race car driver. It's also easy to understand. There aren't a lot of rules that fans have to know in order to be excited. Additionally, the whole family can go to the races together.

Another reason is its humble beginnings. In the 1930s, Bill France was an auto mechanic in Washington, DC. He decided it was too cold in winter to repair cars in his garage. He decided to move to Daytona, Florida. During this time, drivers in Daytona were setting new land-speed records. Then, in 1936, city officials in Daytona decided to sponsor a stock car* race. Bill France raced a car, but he didn't win. The city didn't win either. It lost $22,000 and decided that it would not sponsor any more car races. However, Bill was **convinced** that **eventually** car races could make a lot of money. He was right, but it took him many years of trying to find sponsors and places for cars to race. Finally, in 1947, Bill France and several other car racing **colleagues established** the National Association for Stock Car Racing (NASCAR). Bill France became the first president of the organization. Three months later, the first NASCAR race

*__stock car__—*n.* a standard car that has been changed to be a racing car

was held. NASCAR was on its way, but even Bill probably never dreamed it would get as big as it is today.

Finally, NASCAR is popular because automobiles have a **decades**-long history in the United States. In fact, the first major U.S. manufacturer of cars opened in 1898. Furthermore, a big part of U.S. American **culture** revolves around cars. Getting a drivers' **license** is very important to young people, and most drivers always remember their first cars. Even today, even though the price of gas is rising, Americans love getting out on the open road and just driving.

In short, driving is an important part of U.S. culture. Therefore, it's not surprising that so many enjoy watching the very skilled drivers of NASCAR.

Reading Comprehension

Circle the letter of the correct answer, or write a short answer.

1. According to the reading, how many reasons are there for NASCAR's popularity?
   a. two
   b. three
   c. six
2. Most good race car drivers are natural athletes.
   a. true
   b. false
   c. The reading doesn't say.
3. Why is car racing a good sport for families to enjoy watching together?

   ____
4. Daytona's first stock car race was a success.
   a. true
   b. false
   c. The reading doesn't say.

5. Which of the following statements is NOT true?
   a. Bill France was an auto mechanic in Washington, DC.
   b. Bill France lost $22,000 in Daytona's stock car race in 1936.
   c. Bill France believed that car racing had a future.
6. In 1947, Bill France started NASCAR.
   a. true
   b. false
   c. The reading doesn't say.
7. Why did it take Bill France ten years to establish NASCAR? ________________

   ____
8. In what year was the first NASCAR race held? ______________________
9. Car companies have existed in the U.S. for more than 100 years.
   a. true
   b. false
   c. The reading doesn't say.
10. Why are automobiles such a popular part of U.S. culture?
   a. The U.S. is a big country.
   b. Cars were invented in the United States.
   c. Americans love driving.

Discuss Your Ideas

In small groups, discuss the answers to these questions. Be prepared to share your answers with the class.

1. Have you ever been to a car race? Tell your classmates about the experience.
2. Is the car an important means of transportation in your home city? Why or why not?
3. The reading says that NASCAR is the second-most watched sport on TV in the United States. What do you think is the most watched sport? Why?

STUDY TIP

Reading Transitions Carefully

Be sure to notice transitions while you are reading. They can help you understand the relationships between sentences. Studying them can help you do better on tests if you really understand what the material was teaching.

Vocabulary Comprehension

With a classmate, fill in the empty boxes in the chart below. Do not write anything in the boxes that have an X. You can use an English dictionary.

Nouns	Verbs	Adjectives	Adverbs
	appreciate		
1. colleague 2.	X		X
	convince		
culture	X		
decade	X	X	X
	establish		X
X	X		eventually
license			X

Sentence Completion

Fill in each blank with one of the words from the chart. Use the context to help you choose the correct form of the word.

1. Tony looked for a house for more than a year. He ______________ found one that he and his family liked. It was more expensive than they had hoped, but they still decided to purchase it.
2. Three of my ______________ earned extra money by working on the weekends.
3. In U.S ______________, it is impolite to snap your fingers at anyone.
4. To get married, you need to get a ______________ at city hall. It's only a piece of paper, but you need it for the government to recognize your marriage.
5. Greece was the first country to ______________ a democratic government.

6. In order to be a good leader, you have to give ______________ speeches. People have to believe that you will do what you say.

7. My French teacher is wonderful. I ______________ her clear lessons and the fun activities we do in class.

8. The first 10 years of my life I lived in Tokyo. The next ______________ I lived in Boston in the United States.

Odd One Out

Circle the word that does not belong in each group. Be prepared to explain why the word does not belong.

1. appreciative, grateful, regretful, thankful
2. aunt, colleague, friend, neighbor
3. create, convince, encourage, talk into
4. nature, culture, customs, traditions
5. begin, build, establish, finish
6. at present, eventually, now, currently
7. license, permission, approval, failure
8. century, day, decade, millennium

Vocabulary Use

Vocabulary Note

Some of the target vocabulary in Chapter 14 has usages and meanings that are different from how they were used in the reading. To become a better reader, make sure you understand these phrase/usages:

appreciate *to appreciate in value*

establish *the Establishment* (power structure of a society)

Short Answer

Write an answer to these questions. Try to use the word in bold in your answer.

1. What kind of art did Pablo Picasso **create**? ______________________________
2. How many **decades** does each century have? ___________________________
3. Who gives people marriage **licenses**? _________________________________
4. Who is a **colleague** of a teacher? ____________________________________
5. On Teacher **Appreciation** Day, what do students do? ____________________

   ____

Write about It

Write a paragraph in response to the prompt. Try to use three words from the chart on page 172 in this assignment.

Imagine that you are a race car driver. It is the night before the important race of your career. What are you thinking? What are you hoping for? What are you worried about?

Vocabulary Skill

Skill **Recognizing Word Roots**

Purpose To help you figure out the meaning of words without looking them up a dictionary

Explanation Many words in English are made from Latin and Greek word roots. By learning the word roots, you can often figure out what a word means.

Examples The *ex* in *export* means "out of," and *port* means "carry," so *export* means to carry something out of something or to carry goods out of a country.

The *spec* in *spectator* means "look," and the suffix *or* means a "person," so a *spectator* is a person who looks.

Common Roots	Meaning	Example	Meaning
a, an	not, without	*atypical*	not typical
ben, bene	good	*benefactor*	a person who does good things
bio	life	*biology*	the study of life
cred	believe	*credible*	believable
dict	speak	*diction*	speaking clearly
e, ex	out of	*eject*	throw out
graph	write	*autograph*	signature
mit, mis, miss	send	*emit*	send something out
multi	many	*multicolored*	having many colors
path	feeling	*antipathy*	a feeling of great dislike
port	carry	*portable*	something easy to carry
spec	look	*inspection*	looking at something carefully
tele	far	*television*	a machine that allows you to see something from far away
terr	earth	*territory*	a piece of land
vid, vis	see	*vista*	a beautiful sight

Matching

Match each word in the left column with its probable meaning on the right. Use the word roots to help you. Do not use a dictionary.

____ 1. benefit	a. wonderful to look at
____ 2. biosphere	b. a job that someone is sent away to do
____ 3. credibility	c. the part of the planet where there is life
____ 4. dictate	d. to say something for someone to write down
____ 5. emigrate	e. a good thing
____ 6. envision	f. to see in your mind
____ 7. mission	g. a written message sent far away
____ 8. multitasking	h. to move to another country
____ 9. spectacular	i. doing many things at once
____ 10. telegraph	j. believability

Timed Reading

Read the passage according to your teacher's instructions. Then answer the questions on page 215 without looking at the reading.

A NASCAR Great: Dale Earnhardt

Like any sport, NASCAR has its favorite players. One of the most popular drivers in NASCAR history was Dale Earnhardt. In his 27-year career, he drove in 677 races. Of those, he placed first 76 times. He placed in the top ten finishers 422 times. Some fans loved him, and some fans hated him, but everyone watched him.

Earnhardt grew up as the son of a stock car racer, so he never had a doubt about his future. He knew he would be a race car driver. He started his driving
* career in 1975 and won the title "Rookie of the Year" in 1979. Earnhardt managed to charm audiences with his good looks and personality. He quickly increased the number of NASCAR fans. He was a hard worker and very competitive. He worked diligently to engineer the best cars and then drive them to victory. He also had a good sense of self-promotion. He and his wife started a company called Dale Earnhardt, Inc. His company sells merchandise and also contributes to the charitable organizations that he started.

Earnhardt's life and career came to a tragic end on February 18, 2001. On
* the last lap of the Daytona 500 that year, Dale's car, going at 180 miles per hour, was involved in a multi-car crash on the race track. Earnhardt was killed instantly. The exact cause of the crash is unknown, but Earnhardt may not have been wearing his seatbelt properly. Some fans blamed the other driver in the crash, but Earnhardt's family denied any wrong-doing on that driver's part. The race car world immediately went into mourning. Earnhardt's number 3 was retired, if only temporarily. Moreover, in the months following

Earnhardt's death, fans at NASCAR races held up three fingers in silence as
* the cars drove around the track the third time.

Earnhardt legacy has continued in the years since his death. His son, Dale Earnhardt, Jr., is the third generation of race car drivers in the Earnhardt family. Even before the death of his dad, Dale, Jr. was a race car driver. In fact, he was in the race when his dad died. His company still makes lots of money on his merchandise and still runs the charities Earnhardt started. Also, the millions of people who became NASCAR fans because of Dale Earnhardt are still watching the car races. The senior Dale Earnhardt will not be forgotten.

UNIT 8

A Passion for Nature

Different parts of the world have different types of nature, such as rain forests, deserts, or tropics. Some people have a passion, or a very strong emotion, for nature.

With a classmate, discuss these questions.

1. How many types of nature can you list?
2. Which types of nature have you seen?
3. Which parts of the world have each type of nature?
4. Which type of nature do you like the best? Why?
5. What do you think it means to have a passion for nature? Do you have this passion?

CHAPTER

15

Robert Wyland, Ocean Artist

Getting Ready to Read

A mural is a large wall painting that is usually located outdoors. It is an example of public art that many people can see at one time. With a classmate, answer these questions.

1. Have you ever seen an outdoor mural? Where? What was the subject of the mural?
2. Do you like this kind of art?
3. If you were going to paint a nature mural, what would be in your painting?

Vocabulary Preview

For each sentence, choose one of the words or phrases to match the meaning of the word in bold.

detailed, containing many parts	notice
give attention to	respond
help by giving money or time	something to keep someone safe
natural surroundings	step by step

1. Dolphins and whales can communicate by using **complex** sounds.

   I think **complex** means ______________________________.

2. Many students like to study in quiet libraries because it is easy to **concentrate** there.

   I think **concentrate** means ______________________________.

3. Motorcycle riders often wear helmets for **protection**.

   I think **protection** means ______________________________.

4. Hiking in the mountains is one way to enjoy the **environment.**

   I think **environment** means ______________________________.

5. Most people **react** to funny movies by laughing.

   I think **react** means ______________________________.

6. Your English skills will **gradually** improve if you practice.

   I think **gradually** means ______________________________.

7. If you study sociology, you will **observe** the way humans behave.

   I think **observe** means ______________________________.

8. People who **support** Greenpeace care about the oceans and forests of Earth.

   I think **support** means ______________________________.

Reading Skill

Skill	**Understanding Cause and Effect**
Purpose	To make correct inferences about reasons and results
Example	Look at this sentence from the reading. • **The size of the wall allowed him to create life-size pictures of whales and other ocean animals.**
Explanation	You can infer from this sentence that • **The wall was very big.** (cause) • **He painted life-size ocean animals.** (effect)

Understanding Cause and Effect

Read each sentence, followed by two statements. One is a correct inference, and the other is not. With a classmate, choose the sentence that is the inference. Be prepared to explain your answers.

1. Wyland wants to share the beauty of the ocean with others. He also wants to make people understand that the ocean is a complex part of our environment.
   a. Because the ocean is beautiful, Wyland wants to share it with others.
   b. Because the ocean is a complex part of our environment, people understand it.

2. He decided to become a professional artist and started spending ten hours a day painting. He received a scholarship at the Center for Creative Studies in Detroit, Michigan.
   a. Wyland received a scholarship because he painted ten hours a day.
   b. Because Wyland spent ten hours a day painting, he became a very good painter.

3. In the early 1980s, not many people were interested in ocean art. But gradually, more and more people wanted to buy his paintings, and Wyland learned more about the business of art.
    a. Because people started buying his paintings, Wyland learned more about the business of art.
    b. People started buying his paintings because Wyland learned more about the business of art.
4. His murals show the beauty of ocean life in more than 65 cities in the world. Because of his passion, about one billion people a year have a chance to see and appreciate the undersea world.
    a. One billion people each year view one of Wyland's murals because Wyland has passion for the ocean.
    b. Wyland has passion for the ocean because he has painted murals in 65 countries.

Scanning Practice

Scan the reading for the answers to these questions.

1. How many murals has Robert Wyland painted? ______________________
2. Where did he study painting? ______________________
3. When did he paint the world's largest mural? ______________________
4. Where does he live now?______________________

Reading

Saving the Whales, One Wall at a Time

Robert Wyland is a man with a passion. He loves the undersea world of scuba diving* and all ocean animals, like sharks, whales, dolphins, and colorful fish. Many people think he is the world's most important artist of the ocean. He wants to share the beauty of the ocean with others. He also wants to make people understand that the ocean is a **complex** part of our **environment** and needs our **protection.** For these reasons, Wyland has painted ocean murals in many different cities around the world. In 2008, he painted his 100th mural in Beijing, China.

Wyland's passion began when he was growing up. During the 1970s, there was a popular television show about the ocean scientist Jacques Cousteau. As Wyland watched the great scientist explore the ocean, he became very interested in oceans and all the life in them. When he was a teenager, he went to California to visit an aunt and, for the first time, **observed** a whale swimming in the ocean.

Wyland was already interested in art. He started painting when he was three years old. He later worked in a factory but quickly stopped because he could not **concentrate** on his work. He just wanted to paint. He decided to become a professional artist and starting spending ten hours a day painting. He received a scholarship** to the Center for Creative Studies in Detroit, Michigan. He worked hard in his art with his teachers at the Center.

He returned to California and painted his first mural on the wall of the Laguna Beach Hotel. The size of the wall allowed him to create life-sized

---

*__scuba diving__—*n.* swimming under water while breathing air from a container on your back
**__scholarship__—*n.* money given to a student by an organization to help pay for his/her education

pictures of whales and other ocean animals. The public location of the wall allowed many people to see it. This gave Wyland a chance to watch how people **reacted** to his work. He saw that other people shared his interest in the ocean.

Like many artists, he had problems selling his work at first. In the early 1980s, not many people were interested in ocean art. But **gradually**, more and more people wanted to buy his paintings, and Wyland learned more about the business of art. In 1992, he painted "Planet Ocean," the world's largest mural, in Long Beach, California. This mural is more than 100 feet high and 1,225 feet in diameter.[***] Wyland has also painted other murals in Japan, Australia, Mexico, and France.

Today Wyland enjoys watching ocean animals from his home in Hawaii. He works hard to help **protect** ocean animals from pollution[†] and too much fishing. His organization, the Wyland Foundation, teaches children about the ocean and **supports** the work of ocean scientists. His murals show the beauty of ocean life in more than 65 cities in the world. Because of his passion for the ocean, about one billion people a year have a chance to see and appreciate the undersea world.

[***]**diameter**—*n.* the length of a line passing from one side of a circle to the other

[†]**pollution**—*n.* smoke, chemicals, and other manmade waste making air, water, or land dirty and dangerous for living things

Reading Comprehension

Circle the letter of the correct answer, or write a short answer.

1. Wyland loves the ocean and wants to ________ it.
   a. explore
   b. protect
   c. understand

2. What is the main purpose of Wyland's work?
   a. He wants to use his art for education.
   b. He wants to help people understand the ocean.
   c. He wants to keep traveling.

3. When did Wyland begin painting?
   a. when he was at the Center of Creative Studies
   b. when he was in California
   c. at a very young age

4. As a boy, Wyland lived in California.
   a. true
   b. false
   c. The reading doesn't say.

5. Wyland's murals caused a positive reaction.
   a. true
   b. false
   c. The reading doesn't say.

6. What is "Planet Ocean?" ____

7. The Wyland Foundation gives money to help
   a. educational programs
   b. ocean animals
   c. the creation of murals

8. What are the advantages of the mural as an art form?
   a. It can show art to many people at once.
   b. The artist can observe the public's reaction.
   c. both a and b

9. Which phrase best describes Wyland?
   a. ocean scientist and artist
   b. artist and educator
   c. successful businessman

Discuss Your Ideas

In small groups, discuss the answers to these questions. Be prepared to share your answers with the class.

1. Explain how murals can be a good way to teach people about nature.
2. What are some other ways that murals can be used?
3. Why do you think the Wyland Foundation wants to teach children about the ocean?
4. What kind of work do you have a passion for doing?

STUDY TIP

Managing Stress

Students need to find ways to manage the stress of working hard to reach their goals. Eating healthy food, getting enough sleep, and exercising regularly are important ways to manage stress. It is also helpful to relax and do something fun each day. Talking with friends and family members is another way to manage stress.

Vocabulary Comprehension

With a classmate, fill in the empty boxes in the chart. Do not write anything in the boxes that have an X. You can use an English dictionary.

Nouns	Verbs	Adjectives	Adverbs
	X	complex	X
	concentrate		X
1. environment 2.	X		
X	X		gradually
1. 2.	observe	X	X
1. protection 2.		1. 2.	
reaction			X
1. support 2.			

Matching

Match the words in the left column with their opposite meanings in the right column.

____	1. complex	a. human-made
____	2. concentration	b. ignore
____	3. environmental	c. harm
____	4. gradually	d. distraction
____	5. observe	e. disapproval
____	6. protection	f. suddenly
____	7. react to	g. simple
____	8. support	h. not see

Word Forms

Fill in each blank with one of the words in bold. Use the context to help you choose the correct form of the word.

1. **gradual, gradually**

   The scientists have ____________________ learned more about dolphins.

2. **protection, protectors, protective**

   Wyland believes that ocean animals need our ____________________. We need to become their ____________________.

3. **reaction, react**

   It makes artists happy to see people ____________________ positively to their work.

4. **environment, environmentalist, environmental**

   I worried so much about the ____________________ that I became an ____________________.

5. **concentration, concentrate**

   Some students can ____________________ very well in libraries.

6. **support, supportive, supportively**

   My parents have always been very ____________________ of me. For example, their ____________________ includes paying for my college tuition.

7. **complexity, complex**

   The professor explained the ____________________ math clearly.

8. **observation, observe**

   Parents can learn more about their children when they ____________________ them playing with others.

Vocabulary Use

Vocabulary Note

Some of the target vocabulary in Chapter 15 has usages and meanings that are different from how they were used in the reading. To become a better reader, make sure you understand these phrase/usages:

concentrate *juice made from concentrate* (liquid where some water has been removed); *a concentration of people*

observe *to observe a holiday* (recognize)

True or False

Write T if the statement is true and F if the statement is false.

____ 1. Most adult animals are protective of baby animals.

____ 2. Large windows make the observation of birds more difficult.

____ 3. People sometimes react to loud noises with fear.

____ 4. Different kinds of animals live in different environments.

____ 5. The human body is not very complex.

____ 6. Children do not need financial support from their parents.

____ 7. The sun gradually sets during the evening hours.

____ 8. It's easy for all students to concentrate in a noisy room.

Write about It

Write a paragraph in response to the prompt. Try to use at least three of the words from the chart on page 188 in this assignment.

Wyland received a scholarship to study at an art school. How important is the study of art? Do you think everyone should have a chance to study art, or should only talented people study art?

CHAPTER

16

Saving Luna

Getting Ready to Read

Read each statement. Then check the box that says how you feel about the statement.

	I agree.	I disagree.	I'm not sure.
People are more important than the earth.			
People are more important than animals.			
People are more important than trees.			
A person's relationship to the earth is based on his or her culture.			
My culture respects the earth.			

Discuss your opinions with a small group. How are they similar? How are they different?

Vocabulary Preview

For each sentence, choose one of the words or phrases to match the meaning of the word in bold.

form of communication	stay
familiar with	trade
places to live	very big
set up	worthwhile

1. Our new house has an **enormous** backyard. My children are not **accustomed to** having a big backyard because our old home was an apartment.

   I think **enormous** means ________________________________.

   I think **accustomed to** means ________________________________.

2. Presidential press conferences are covered by many kinds of **media**. You can see reporters from cable shows, newspapers, and magazines. When the President walks in the room, everyone stops talking. They **remain** quiet until the President asks for questions.

   I think **media** means ________________________________.

   I think **remain** means ________________________________.

3. House "swapping" is becoming more popular because it is less expensive than traditional vacations. House swapping is when two people **exchange residences** for a week or more. Each person can stay for free and visit a new place.

   Some people swap residences in remote locations.

   I think **exchange** means ________________________________.

   I think **residences** means ________________________________.

4. My daughter and I watched an interesting interview on the news last night. The reporter was talking with a man and his daughter. Together, they **founded** an organization to help young girls in poor countries go to school. Watching this interview was **valuable** for my daughter because she is interested in the same kind of work.

   I think **founded** means ____.

   I think **valuable** means ____.

Reading Skill

Skill	**Distinguishing Facts, Opinions, and Unknowns**
Purpose	To increase understanding of a reading
Explanation	*Facts* are stated directly in the reading text. Facts are pieces of true information. They are sometimes related to size, amount, or number. Facts can sometimes be inferred. (To infer is to make a good guess using the information that you have.) *Opinions* are what someone thinks. Other people can agree or disagree. *Unknowns* are not stated at all in the reading text.
Example	**The forest used to be enormous and covered most of the northwestern part of the United States.** • **The forest is in the northwestern part of the United States.** (Fact) • **The forest is smaller than it used to be.** (Inferred Fact; we can guess this is true because it says that the forest used to be enormous.) • **The forest was very beautiful.** (Opinion) • **Many kinds of animals lived in the forest.** (Unknown)

Fact, Opinion, or Unknown?

Read these sentences from the reading. Then read each sentence that follows. Write F if it is a fact, O if it is an opinion, or U if it is an unknown.

1. Like many people, Julia thought that these trees were valuable and should never be cut down.

    _____ These trees were valuable.

    _____ There is one main reason for cutting down these trees.

    _____ Other people thought the trees were valuable.

2. Julia's life in the tree was difficult, but she became accustomed to it.

    _____ It wasn't easy for Julia to live in the tree.

    _____ It is crazy to live in a tree.

    _____ It took a long time for Julia to get used to living in her tree.

3. Julia was alone in her tree most of the time, but a few people visited her.

    _____ Julia loved having visitors in her tree.

    _____ Julia had visitors when she lived in her tree.

    _____ It was surprising that Julia had visitors in her tree.

Reading

Julia Butterfly Hill

When Julia Hill was 23 years old, she climbed up an old redwood tree and stayed there for more than two years. People said she was crazy, but she had a good reason to stay in the tree. She didn't want the lumber company to cut the tree down.

During her time in the tree, Julia changed her name to Julia Butterfly, and she named her tree Luna. Luna was one of many trees in the Headwaters Forest. This forest is about 230 miles north of San Francisco. The Pacific Lumber Company owned Headwaters Forest and wanted to cut down the trees. However, these trees were very old. In fact, some of them were more than 1,000 years old. This forest used to be **enormous** and covered most of the northwestern part of the United States. But now, only about three percent of the forest **remains**. Like many people, Julia thought that these trees were **valuable** and should never be cut down. So, she climbed a tree. She knew that the lumber company would not cut down the tree if she were on top of it.

Julia had two levels in her tree. One level was at 100 feet, and the other one was at 180 feet. Her "rooms" were only 4 feet by 6 feet. Because it rains a lot in Northern California, she had tarps* on tops of the rooms to keep her dry. She got her food and supplies from a friend who would send them up in a basket with a rope. In short, Julia's life in the tree was difficult, but she became **accustomed to** it.

* **tarp**—*n.* a large plastic covering

Sometimes Julia had visitors but not often. Most people didn't want to climb 100 feet! However, she had many phone interviews with the **media**. Also, many people from around the world wrote letters to her, and she answered every one. So, while Julia was alone most of the time, she still had contact with people.

Finally, after 738 days, the Pacific Lumber Company and Julia came to an agreement. The lumber company promised not to cut down Luna or any of the trees around Luna. In **exchange**, Julia agreed to come down and pay $50,000 to the company for living in the tree for two years. When Julia finally came down, her father gave her a big hug. He was very proud of her. She saw a problem and did something to make it better.

Today, Julia is a famous spokesperson for the environmental movement. With a colleague, she **founded** an organization to help small groups of people make environmental and social changes. She has written several books. One is about her two-year **residence** in Luna. She also has a popular blog, where fans can keep track of what she's doing. It's clear that Julia Butterfly Hill is still trying to protect the environment, but she now does it with her two feet on the ground!

Reading Comprehension

Circle the letter of the correct answer, or write a short answer.

1. Julia climbed up Luna because she wanted to become a famous environmentalist.
   a. true
   b. false
   c. The reading doesn't say.
2. Julia changed her name
   a. while she was living in Luna.
   b. before she lived in Luna.
   c. after she lived in Luna.
3. Luna is probably more than 1,000 years old.
   a. true
   b. false
   c. The reading doesn't say.
4. Who owned Luna when Julia lived there? ______________________________
5. The Headwater Forest used to be much smaller.
   a. true
   b. false
   c. The reading doesn't say.
6. Julia's "rooms"
   a. were next to each other.
   b. were enormous.
   c. were at least 100 feet in the air.
7. How did Julia get food and supplies? ______________________________
8. While she was in her tree, Julia
   a. talked on the phone and wrote letters.
   b. had many visitors.
   c. was very lonely.

9. Pacific Lumber Company paid Julia $50,000 to come down from the tree.
   a. true
   b. false
   c. The reading doesn't say.

10. What has Julia done since she came down from Luna? ____________________

____

Discuss Your Ideas

In small groups, discuss the answers to these questions. Be prepared to share your answers with the class.

1. Why do you think Julia Hill changed her name to Julia Butterfly?
2. Why do you think Julia gave a name to the tree she lived in?
3. Julia's actions are an example of how one person can make a difference in a situation. Do you know of any other situations where one person made a difference? Explain it.

STUDY TIP

Forming Study Groups

Study groups are informal groups of students who meet on a regular basis in order to study together. They discuss the notes they take in class and the readings for the class. They also help each other with homework and studying for tests. This can be a valuable learning experience for native and non-native speakers of English. When you get to a college or university, try to find a study group, or establish one yourself.

Vocabulary Comprehension

With a classmate, fill in the empty boxes in the chart. Do not write anything in the boxes that have an X. You can use an English dictionary.

Nouns	Verbs	Adjectives	Adverbs
X	X	accustomed	X
	X	enormous	
exchange			X
1. 2.	found	X	X
media (medium)	X	X	X
	remain		X
1. residence 2.			X
		valuable	X

Sentence Completion

Fill in each blank with one of the words from the chart on page 200. Use the context to help you choose the correct form of the word.

1. It seems that the _______________ of gold _______________ the same through good economic times and bad economic times. The price is always good.
2. My family's construction company was _______________ 100 years ago. It started as a small company with my two uncles.
3. It seems that reporters from different _______________ organizations often move from one news organization to another.
4. I live in an _______________ apartment building. There are 100 apartments and 300 _______________ who live there.
5. When you move to another country, it may take a while to become _______________ to the culture and customs. Sometimes, it's helpful to find someone for a language _______________. This person and you can help each other by taking turns speaking two languages.

Odd One Out

Circle the word that does not belong in each group. Be prepared to explain why the word does not belong.

1. accustomed, familiar, unknown, used to
2. enormous, little, small, tiny
3. exchange, get rid of, give away, sell
4. build, destroy, establish, found
5. diary, newspaper, radio, television
6. leave, remain, stay, wait
7. guest, resident, tourist, visitor
8. cheap, inexpensive, useless, valuable

Vocabulary Use

Vocabulary Note

Some of the target vocabulary in Chapter 16 has usages and meanings that are different from how they were used in the reading. To become a better reader, make sure you understand these phrase/usages:

media the singular form is *medium* (*visit a medium*)

remain *someone's remains* (someone's body after death; always used in the plural).

Short Answer

Write an answer to these questions. Try to use the word in bold in your answer.

1. List these animals in order of their **enormity:** elephant, frog, monkey, tiger.

   ____

2. List these items in order of their **value:** bicycle, camera, car, house.

   ____

3. Are there more **residents** in urban areas or in rural areas?

   ____

4. When you travel to a foreign country, what do you need to **exchange**?

   ____

5. How long do summer residents of a beach area **remain** in their summer home?

   ____

Write about It

Write a paragraph in response to the prompt. Try to use three words from the chart on page 200.

Imagine a day in the life of Julia Butterfly when she was living in her tree. Write a diary of a typical day for her from the time she wakes up to the time she goes to sleep.

Vocabulary Skill

Skill — **Using Word Roots and Affixes to Understand the Meanings of Words in Context**

Purpose — To spend less time looking words up in a dictionary and more time reading

Explanation — You can use your knowledge of word roots and affixes to figure out the meaning of a sentence or a passage.

Example — **After finding the *subterranean* piece of *evidence,* the sheriff knew he would have to *revise* his theory of who the killer was.**

1. Where was the *evidence* found?

   Sub means "under" and *terr* means "earth."

   The answer is "underground."

2. What happened next?

   Re means "again," *vis* means "see," and *spec* means "look."

   The answer is that the sheriff changed the way he looked at something.

True or False

Read the passage.

Joey South: A Biography

Joey South led an unusual life. Even his childhood was **atypical**. He grew up on an ostrich ranch in Arizona, where his mother taught him to read and his father taught him to care for ostriches.

When Joey left the ranch at age 20, he became a tourist guide in the Arctic Circle. He led people over the cold **terrain**. He said the tourists became his **benefactors**. By the time he left, he had earned a lot of money. Then, he went to work in a circus as a **telepath**. He said that it wasn't difficult making predictions about what people were thinking because most people think about similar things. At one point in his life, Joey became a **missionary** and went to the South Pacific. During those years, he was healthy and happy. He left when the government changed and issued an **edict** demanding that all foreigners leave.

Joey always said that the most interesting job he had was as a **stenographer**. Every day, he listened to lawyers talk to witnesses, present the **evidence,** and try to persuade the jury. He would type it on his **portable** steno* machine and then take it home to make it readable to the lawyers. He said it made him glad that he never got into trouble with the law.

Joey South died in his sleep at age 91. He left behind a loving wife, two daughters, and five grandchildren. More than 100 people attended the memorial service of this **incredible** man.

***steno**—*prefix.* making something shorter

Read the statements. Write T if the statement is true and F if it is false. Use your knowledge of word roots in the bold words in the reading to help you.

____ 1. As an adult, Joey's life was different than most people's lives, but his childhood was similar.

____ 2. As a tourist guide, Joey organized walking tours on a ship in the Arctic.

____ 3. The tourists on the ship liked Joey.

____ 4. In the circus, Joey worked as a mind reader.

____ 5. In the South Pacific, Joey didn't meet many people.

____ 6. Joey left the South Pacific because he wanted to.

____ 7. In court, Joey was responsible for writing down what people said.

____ 8. The lawyers showed things to the jury.

____ 9. His steno machine was light enough to carry.

____ 10. The writer of the story thinks that Joey was an average man.

Timed Reading

Read the passage according to your teacher's instructions. Then answer the questions on page 216 without looking at the reading.

Deep Sea Creatures

Recently, scientists discovered new deep sea animals in the Weddell Sea near Antarctica. They found urchins, sponges, and ten-inch wide sea spiders. In all, seven hundred previously unknown sea creatures were discovered at a depth of nearly 20,000 feet. The variety of species there surprised scientists because it is believed that life at that depth is so hard that there is only a limited variety that could survive. However, even creatures that live below only 1,000 feet have had to adapt to deep sea living in many ways.

Sea creatures at such depths live under incredible pressure from the * weight of the water. Consequently, their bones and muscles are soft and flexible, and they don't have a lot of extra space in their bodies. Any extra space would collapse under the pressure.

A major difficulty for these animals is finding food. Most of their food comes from above when bits and pieces of other animals fall down. In addition, many fish have huge mouths and stomachs which allow them to consume fish larger than themselves. Another way of attracting prey for food is through luminescence, or light. Deep sea fish, such as the angler, have internal * organs that can produce light when a food fish is near.

Creatures living at these levels must be careful that they themselves don't become food. So, through time, they have developed strategies to protect themselves. Some species have developed ways of camouflaging themselves so that they blend into the background. For example, the crocodile ice fish is transparent, so it is difficult to see. Still other fish are black and easily blend in with the background. Red fish also blend into the background well because red becomes black below 7,500 feet.

Deep sea creatures have also developed other interesting ways of protecting themselves from predators. One way is by using electricity. Some creatures can sense the electric fields of prey as they move through the water. Some other creatures, such as the sting ray, can actually produce electricity to shock their enemies into fleeing. Another way fish have to protect themselves is by using venom. These types of creatures usually have spines which conduct the poison into the enemy.

Like the new animals found at extreme ocean depths near Antarctica, deep sea creatures worldwide have adapted perfectly to their environment over the millennia. And their adaptations continue to astonish both scientists and amateur biologists.

Appendix 1: Timed Reading Questions

Unit 1 Timed Reading

Write T if the statement is true and F if the statement is false.

____ 1. Hip hop began in a New York neighborhood in the 1970s.

____ 2. In the 1970s, the Bronx was a good place to live.

____ 3. Jamaican music influenced the development of hip hop music.

____ 4. The most important rap instrument is the voice.

____ 5. DJs play rap on the radio.

____ 6. Michael Jackson was one of the original hip hop dancers.

____ 7. Hip hop dancers have to be very strong.

____ 8. To be a hip hop dancer, you must develop your own moves.

____ 9. In some hip hop dancing, your feet are not on the ground.

____ 10. Hip hop music and dance only happens in the United States.

Unit 2 Timed Reading

Write T if the statement is true and F if the statement is false.

_____ 1. All of the Triple Crown Trails go north-south.

_____ 2. The oldest trail is in the western part of the U.S.

_____ 3. Thru-hikers complete all three trails in one year.

_____ 4. The longest goes through the middle of the country.

_____ 5. Hikers deal with the greatest variety of weather on the Pacific Crest Trail.

_____ 6. The Pacific Crest trail starts in Mexico and ends in Canada.

_____ 7. The Continental Divide trail is the most difficult to thru-hike.

_____ 8. Altitude sickness can be dangerous.

_____ 9. The trails are so well marked that hikers do not need compasses.

_____ 10. Completing a thru-hike takes time, but it is not difficult.

Unit 3 Timed Reading

Write T if the statement is true and F if the statement is false.

_____ 1. Alaska and Hawaii became part of the United States in the same year.

_____ 2. The United States purchased Alaska and Hawaii in the 1800s.

_____ 3. There are more Alaskans than there are Hawaiians.

_____ 4. Alaska has less than one million people.

_____ 5. During the winter, Alaska can be dark for twenty hours a day.

_____ 6. Hawaii's climate is perfect for indoor activities.

_____ 7. Most people in Hawaii descended from the original native population.

_____ 8. Most Alaskans are descended from the non-native population.

_____ 9. Hawaii's temperature doesn't vary as much as Alaska's.

_____ 10. Alaskans are more active indoors during the summer than they are during the winter.

Unit 4 Timed Reading

Write T if the statement is true and F if the statement is false.

____ 1. Working with animals is a dream of many adults.

____ 2. Working with animals is fun and easy.

____ 3. Wild animal trainers usually don't go to college because they learn on the job.

____ 4. Trainers don't need to worry about an animal attacking them after working with it for a long time.

____ 5. Many trainers volunteer before they find a paying job.

____ 6. It can be dangerous to be a wild animal trainer.

____ 7. Animal trainers need physical strength as well as knowledge.

____ 8. Most animal trainers are shy and work better with animals than with people.

____ 9. Wild animals are fast learners.

____ 10. For a wild animal to learn a trick, it has to repeat the trick many times.

Unit 5 Timed Reading

Write T if the statement is true and F if the statement is false.

____ 1. The Touareg people live in South America.

____ 2. The Festival of the Desert has existed for centuries.

____ 3. The Festival takes place in the Sahara Desert.

____ 4. The musicians at the festival are from all over the world.

____ 5. The musicians play all day and all night.

____ 6. The Touareg music played at the Festival is very traditional.

____ 7. The Touareg people are called the blue people because they play desert blues.

____ 8. The world has become more aware of the Touareg people and their problems because of the festival.

____ 9. Touareg musicians play electric guitars.

____ 10. Unemployment is a problem for young Touareg people.

Unit 6 Timed Reading

Write T if the statement is true and F if the statement is false.

_____ 1. Apple pies are very popular in the United States.

_____ 2. Apples did not grow in North America until the 1600s.

_____ 3. The first settlers used apples for making cider, not for making pies.

_____ 4. The legend of Johnny Appleseed is based on a true story.

_____ 5. The Greeks and Romans made the first apple pies.

_____ 6. Pie crusts were considered better tasting than the inside of the pie itself.

_____ 7. The first pies were meat pies.

_____ 8. The colonists brought the idea of state fairs with them from England.

_____ 9. At the first state fairs, there were only animals and produce displayed.

_____ 10. Pie-eating contests were part of the first fairs.

Unit 7 Timed Reading

Write T if the statement is true and F if the statement is false.

____ 1. Everyone, fans and drivers, loved Dale Earnhardt, Sr.

____ 2. Earnhardt became a race car driver because his father was a mechanic.

____ 3. Because of Earnhardt, more people started watching car races.

____ 4. Earnhardt drove cars that other people engineered.

____ 5. Earnhardt earned money by selling self-promoting merchandise.

____ 6. Earnhardt's death saddened the race car world for many months.

____ 7. Earnhardt died at work.

____ 8. Earnhardt died because of a driving mistake.

____ 9. Earnhardt's son has the same job as his father and grandfather had.

____ 10. Earnhardt's family still makes a lot of money from his legacy.

Unit 8 Timed Reading

Write T if the statement is true and F if the statement is false.

____ 1. Previously unknown deep sea creatures were recently found in the Arctic Sea.

____ 2. The variety of animals that were found surprised scientists.

____ 3. Life for deep sea creatures is difficult in many ways.

____ 4. Deep sea animals have adapted to be able to survive the pressure of the ocean.

____ 5. One adaptation is that their bones are very strong and hard.

____ 6. Most deep sea animals find other deep sea animals to kill and eat.

____ 7. Some deep sea fish attract prey by making light inside their bodies.

____ 8. Red, black and transparent fish can easily hide from predator fish.

____ 9. Fish that produce electricity kill the fish they want to eat.

____ 10. Some deep sea creatures use venom to capture food fish.

Appendix 2: Increasing Reading Speed

Timed Reading

Timed reading is a very common activity in language classes. In this exercise, you read a passage at your own pace, record your time when you finish, and then answer the questions.

Timed Reading Procedure

1. Read the passage faster than you normally would. As you are reading, your teacher will be writing the amount of time that passes on the board.
2. Look up when you are finished, and note the time it took you to read the entire passage.
3. Answer the questions without looking back at the passage.
4. When everyone in the class is finished, your teacher will go over the answers.
5. Determine the percentage of correct answers you got.
6. Fill in the **Timed Reading Chart** on page 219 by putting a dot at the intersection of the unit number and the time it took you to read the passage. Connect the dots with each reading you do. You should try to read a little faster every time. Put the score that you got on the comprehension questions in the box below the unit number.

Note to teacher: Start all the students at the same time. For every ten seconds that elapse, write the time on the board. For example, you would write: 0:10, 0:20, 0:30, etc. Continue in this manner until all the students have completed the passage.

Paced Reading

Paced reading is a very effective fast-reading activity because it clearly demonstrates that you can read fast and still understand a lot. In this activity, the whole class is reading at the same pace. The teacher sets the pace, which is regularly increased.

Before you start, you need to look at one of the passages. At the left-hand side of the reading, there are three stars. These stars mark off 100-word segments to the reading.

Paced Reading Procedure

1. Do not start reading the passage until your teacher tells you to start.
2. When you hear your teacher say "star," look out of the corner of your eye and find the first star in the margin. If you are behind, skip to that point in the reading and continue reading. If you are ahead of the first "star," continue reading where you are.
3. Follow the same procedure each time your teacher says "star."
4. When your teacher says "stop reading," turn to the questions and answer them without looking back at the reading.
5. When everyone in the class is finished, your teacher will go over the answers.
6. Determine the percentage of correct answers you got.
7. Fill in the **Paced Reading Chart** onn page 220 by putting a dot at the intersection of the unit number and your score. Connect the dots with each reading you do.
8. Your teacher will tell you the pace at which the class was reading. Write the pace in the box below the unit number.

Note to teacher: Start the students at the same time. Use this chart to determine when you say "star" to set the pace you want.

WPM	Say "star" every	WPM	Say "star" every	WPM	Say "star" every
100	60 seconds	225	26 seconds	325	18 seconds
125	48 seconds	250	24 seconds	350	17 seconds
150	40 seconds	275	22 seconds	375	16 seconds
175	34 seconds	300	20 seconds	400	15 seconds
200	30 seconds				

Timed Reading Chart

Unit	1	2	3	4	5	6	7	8
Score								
1:00 400 wpm								
1:10 345 wpm								
1:20 300 wpm								
1:30 265 wpm								
1:40 240 wpm								
1:50 220 wpm								
2:00 200 wpm								
2:10 185 wpm								
2:20 170 wpm								
2:30 160 wpm								
2:40 150 wpm								
2:50 140 wpm								
3:00 135 wpm								
3:10 125 wpm								
3:20 120 wpm								
3:40 110 wpm								
3:50 105 wpm								
4:00 100 wpm								

Paced Reading Chart

Unit		1	2	3	4	5	6	7	8
Pace									
Score	100								
	90								
	80								
	70								
	60								
	50								
	40								
	30								
	20								
	10								
	0								

Appendix 3: Index of Target Words

Words from the Academic Word List are starred.
The chapter numbers are in parentheses after each word.